T0248228

GET
GROWING

DEAN SEDDON GET GROWING

GET CLIENTS, GROW FASTER, AND SPEND LESS TIME SELLING

WILEY

Copyright © 2024 by John Wiley & Sons, Inc. All rights reserved.

Published by John Wiley & Sons, Inc., Hoboken, New Jersey.
Published simultaneously in Canada.

No part of this publication may be reproduced, stored in a retrieval system, or transmitted in any form or by any means, electronic, mechanical, photocopying, recording, scanning, or otherwise, except as permitted under Section 107 or 108 of the 1976 United States Copyright Act, without either the prior written permission of the Publisher, or authorization through payment of the appropriate per-copy fee to the Copyright Clearance Center, Inc., 222 Rosewood Drive, Danvers, MA 01923, (978) 750-8400, fax (978) 750-4470, or on the web at www.copyright.com. Requests to the Publisher for permission should be addressed to the Permissions Department, John Wiley & Sons, Inc., 111 River Street, Hoboken, NJ 07030, (201) 748-6011, fax (201) 748-6008, or online at http://www.wiley.com/go/permission.

Limit of Liability/Disclaimer of Warranty: While the publisher and author have used their best efforts in preparing this book, they make no representations or warranties with respect to the accuracy or completeness of the contents of this book and specifically disclaim any implied warranties of merchantability or fitness for a particular purpose. No warranty may be created or extended by sales representatives or written sales materials. The advice and strategies contained herein may not be suitable for your situation. You should consult with a professional where appropriate. Further, readers should be aware that websites listed in this work may have changed or disappeared between when this work was written and when it is read. Neither the publisher nor authors shall be liable for any loss of profit or any other commercial damages, including but not limited to special, incidental, consequential, or other damages.

For general information on our other products and services or for technical support, please contact our Customer Care Department within the United States at (800) 762-2974, outside the United States at (317) 572-3993 or fax (317) 572-4002.

Wiley also publishes its books in a variety of electronic formats. Some content that appears in print may not be available in electronic formats. For more information about Wiley products, visit our web site at www.wiley.com.

Library of Congress Cataloging-in-Publication Data:

Names: Seddon, Dean, author.
Title: Get growing : get clients, grow faster, and spend less time selling
  / Dean Seddon.
Description: Hoboken, New Jersey : Wiley, [2024] | Includes index.
Identifiers: LCCN 2023046856 (print) | LCCN 2023046857 (ebook) | ISBN
  9781394205844 (cloth) | ISBN 9781394205868 (adobe pdf) | ISBN
  9781394205851 (epub)
Subjects: LCSH: Small business—Growth. | Small business marketing. |
  Self-employed.
Classification: LCC HD62.7 .S425 2024 (print) | LCC HD62.7 (ebook) | DDC
  658.4/06—dc23/eng/20231207
LC record available at https://lccn.loc.gov/2023046856
LC ebook record available at https://lccn.loc.gov/2023046857

Cover Design and Image: Wiley

SKY10063687_010324

To adversity and consistency, the unsung heroes
of our growth and progress

Contents

Introduction

At the age of 17, the world of business captivated me with its allure of entrepreneurial autonomy and unlimited potential. The idea of becoming my own boss, charting my own path was an intoxicating vision that spurred me to dive headfirst into starting my own business. Nothing was going to stop me. For every obstacle I would find a solution. I was too young to open a business bank account, so I settled for using my student bank account. Maybe foolish looking back, but nothing could deter me. I was brimming with enthusiasm and that carried me past each hurdle.

I ventured into offering design and printing services to businesses. Looking back, I'm not sure the idea itself was that exciting, but it was the first real idea I came across. Any business would have got me excited back then. I chose my business name, designed my logo, and set up my domain name and email. The internet was pretty new in 1999, it was all dial-up, but I got a single page up online. I also got myself an impressive batch of business cards ready to hand out to the hundreds of people who would want to do business with me.

I was open for business. And nothing happened.

I dropped leaflets around industrial estates, showed up at networking events, put in tireless efforts to drum up business, yet the phone remained eerily silent. A question gnawed at me: "Why is this so hard?" After all, I could see the potential in my business, so why couldn't others?

I did land some business deals, even a few significant ones. Yet they were random victories in what felt like a continuous uphill battle. Some people called up and asked for quotes, but the success was hit and miss because most people wanted it cheaper. I did do okay when customers needed a rush job. And I picked up one client who was an absolute dream and I felt lucky to have them. They became my biggest customer. They spent $5k a month, and this was in the '90s.

Two years in, I made the hard decision to call it quits. My dream client went out of business and I didn't have much else in the pipeline. The steady lack of business, combined with my dream client's bankruptcy (and their unpaid invoices), left me in a financial mess. The entrepreneurial journey ended with me deep in debt.

The failure was a harsh blow, not just to my wallet but to my spirit. I was left feeling wounded and embarrassed, and the failure was traumatic to my mental health. In the aftermath, I spent months licking my wounds. But I needed money. I needed a job. So I had to go job hunting. The irony? I was now working for a company that I owed money to from my failed venture. Every person there knew about my debt, an uncomfortable reality that weighed heavily on me. But they gave me a chance—a chance to pay them back and get back on my feet.

But what might have turned into a daunting experience turned out to be my lifeline. The team at the company was nothing short of supportive and patient. They did not see me as a failure but as a fellow worker with potential. Over the course of two years, not only did I manage to clear my debts, but I also acquired invaluable knowledge and experience about running a successful business. The company had extended more than just a job opportunity; they had given me a chance to grow, learn, and heal.

Despite this, I knew I couldn't remain there forever. My identity, tarnished by the public memory of my failure, was a feeling I carried every day at work. I had to escape that stifling feeling. So I decided to move on—not out of ingratitude, but out of a need to find my own path again.

The experience taught me the crux of the issue that led to my business's downfall: sales, or rather the lack thereof. Funny how that story sparked my 24-year journey of learning how to master sales across different industries, verticals, and types of businesses. The struggle that brought my business down became almost a mission for me to help others. Along this journey, I've met thousands of business owners struggling with the same issues I faced, asking the same questions, "How do I get clients?" "How can I grow faster?"

Sales and marketing are critical to the success of a business. Nobody starts a business intending to become a salesperson or a marketer. Most start because they have a unique idea and a desire to share it with the world. But without sales and marketing, those great ideas are just dreams. The ability to attract new clients and grow a business is not a nice-to-have; it's a necessity. It's the lifeblood that sustains and fuels a business.

Unfortunately, many business owners find themselves overwhelmed with the demands of sales and marketing, from the hours spent crafting social media posts to writing sales copy. I've seen a common pattern in many small businesses. They start from passion and build from a personal network. Most small businesses rely on the network and connections of their founder. I've met a number of ex-corporate execs who have started businesses and thrived because they were well connected. This gives them a network to work, to get the business off the ground. As time goes on that network gets dry, so more and more the business has to rely on marketing and sales to get clients and grow. That's when a business is really tested. For many, their business has had the backing of the founders' connections and network to get a hearing with prospects, but eventually the baby has to stand solely on its own two feet.

That's when you need a strong strategy to attract, nurture, and convert clients.

Looking at the media's portrayal of businesses, one might think that the economy rests solely on the shoulders of large, global corporations. Billion-dollar deals and venture capital funding dominate the headlines, overshadowing the reality that small businesses form the backbone of our economy. As of now, more than 90% of global employment is generated by small businesses. These are not just statistics; these businesses are the life force that keep our communities thriving.

This book is not intended for multi-billion-dollar companies. It's for the tireless entrepreneur working late into the night, the business owner juggling multiple roles, the innovator navigating the maze of self-marketing. It's for those who believe in the power of their ideas and work tirelessly to bring them to fruition.

The prosperity of our nations and our societies is linked intrinsically with the success of small businesses. A small business that grows and expands can provide employment, give others a chance, and help a community flourish. Small businesses can give second, third, and fourth chances to people that corporate hiring managers often can't. Small businesses may be overlooked in the media, but they are key to the prosperity of our community.

I know firsthand the pain of trying to market and promote a business. I know the frustration of fruitless efforts, the sinking feeling of impossibility. I've experienced the disappointment when your idea doesn't find the reception you hoped for. But I've also heard incredible success stories of ordinary people building extraordinary businesses that make a difference in their communities.

When I first started my own business, I didn't anticipate the challenges that would come with sales and marketing. It seemed like an uphill battle, and I often found myself questioning the best way to sell my services. I would daily overthink every aspect of the sales process, leaving me feeling overwhelmed and unsure of the most effective strategies to attract clients.

One of the biggest struggles all small businesses face is getting leads and inquiries. It's frustrating when you know the value of your service but people don't see it. You pour your heart and soul into your business, passionate about making a difference in the lives of your clients. Yet, despite your best efforts, you find yourself struggling to attract the right kind of inquiries and leads from clients who truly value what you offer.

You want to spend less time on marketing and selling, and more time doing what you love. But it seems like it's a never-ending, all-consuming task. After all, that's why you started your business in the first place: to pursue your passion and make a meaningful impact. But the reality is that marketing and selling consume a significant portion of your time and energy, leaving you with less time to focus on the core activities that you're truly passionate about.

The good news is that you're not alone in this journey.

There are countless small business owners and solopreneurs who share the same struggles and desires as you do. They want to overcome the obstacles that come with marketing and selling our services effectively. They want to connect with clients who appreciate the value we provide and are willing to invest in our offerings.

Imagine a world where your marketing efforts effortlessly attract the right clients, those who understand the true worth of your services and eagerly seek your expertise. How much time would you get back if you could systemize your client acquisition? In the pages of this book, I will share practical insights, strategies, and mindset shifts that will empower you to overcome the challenges of marketing and selling. We'll explore ways to effectively communicate the value of your services, attract leads that align with your vision, and streamline your marketing efforts to accelerate growth.

For the last decade, I've been imparting the principles enclosed in this book to entrepreneurs worldwide. I've watched businesses prosper and lives change thanks to these strategies. I've shared ways of thinking that can simplify and demystify the sales and marketing process for small businesses.

It's time to unleash the potential that lies within your business and discover the secrets to marketing and selling your services in a way that aligns with your values and goals.

"How do I get clients, grow faster, and spend less time selling?"

This is the handbook I wish I could have sent back in time to my ambitious 17-year-old self, and the guide I hope will help countless entrepreneurs avoid the pitfalls I encountered.

This book is my contribution to a world full of dreamers, innovators, and tireless workers who want to take their ideas to the world.

Chapter 1

Changing the World with Outcomes

Back in the days of my fledgling printing business, I tried my hand at every marketing tactic that I could lay my hands on. From old-school leaflet drops to making connections at networking events, sending out marketing faxes, and even the somewhat daunting cold calling, I threw myself into the task headfirst. It was certainly no walk in the park.

With meticulous effort, I designed a portfolio of polished marketing materials to showcase our outstanding printing and design services. Yet, despite the creativity and thought put into each piece, the response was disappointingly tepid.

The scanty clientele I did manage to attract fell into two distinct categories: those who had been let down elsewhere and required an urgent service, and the bargain hunters looking for a lower price. These two groups eventually formed the bulk of my inquiries. Yet the individuals seeking exceptional design and superior quality printing—the exact offerings we prided ourselves on—were conspicuously absent. The focus, it seemed, was primarily on speed and affordability.

Looking at other businesses in the locality that had been around for longer, I couldn't help but wonder about their success. They were charging significantly higher prices, and yet they seemed to be doing incredibly well. I found myself grappling with an enigma.

Why would people choose to pay more to purchase from them? I was just as visible, promoting my services just as hard. Yet something was missing.

As I delved deeper, it dawned on me. I was showcasing my services, but I wasn't clarifying why people should choose me. The clients I attracted were driven by two motivations: speed and affordability. They were reaching out because their needs hadn't been met elsewhere. Having come across my marketing material, they decided to reach out to see if I could offer them what they needed: either a faster service or a cheaper one.

It was only years later, with the benefit of hindsight and a deeper understanding of business dynamics, that I could connect the dots. I understood why I consistently attracted only two types of inquiries. It was a fundamental revelation, as simple as it was profound: people buy outcomes. The desire for an outcome—whether faster service, lower price, or something else—drives their purchasing decisions. It's not just about what you offer, but how it transforms their current situation. That, in essence, is the key.

A Vehicle of Transformation

Not long ago, I found myself sifting through a collection of old boxes filled with artifacts from the early days of my business. Among these relics was a marketing leaflet from 1999. Glancing at the cover, I noticed three promotional prices for printed stationery, prominently displayed for potential clients. My contact details and a list of our additional services graced the back, along with the enticing offer of a 24-hour turnaround service.

As I looked at this old piece of marketing, I realized that, albeit unintentionally, this leaflet was perfectly crafted to appeal to individuals who needed their printing done either urgently or on a budget. A nostalgic smile formed on my face, reminding me of countless inquiries from people in need of promotional marketing materials, who had either been let down by their regular supplier or simply lacked the necessary budget to afford their prices.

It brought into sharp focus a powerful lesson that's applicable across all sectors, whether you're dealing in accountancy, technology, or any other service. At the core of every purchase lies a transformation, a transition from their present state to a desired future one. This is the underlying motivation that drives every client, irrespective of who they are. From the CEO of a multinational corporation to the janitor maintaining the premises, each and every one of them buys outcomes, not just the product or service itself.

I realized that the most successful businesses sell transformation.

What customers are really buying is not just the product or service; it's the outcomes they anticipate those products or services will deliver. These outcomes often coincide with their desire to improve their current state or to resolve a pressing issue. They aren't just purchasing a service; they are investing in a promise, a promise of a specific outcome that will propel them closer to their goals or help them navigate a challenging situation. It's an understanding of this fundamental concept that forms the bedrock of effective marketing and sales.

The world of business is teeming with companies offering a myriad of products and services. However, when you peel back the layers of marketing jargon and promotional fluff, the core principle that underpins every transaction becomes clear. It's not about the product or service itself; it's about the outcome it delivers. In essence, every service or product is a tool, a vehicle that transports the customer from their current state to a future, more desirable one. (See Figure 1.1.)

Take a simple gym membership, for instance. People don't purchase a gym membership to gain access to rows of treadmills and weight racks; they're investing in the promise of improved health,

Current State

Point A

Future State

Point B

Your Service

Sell the DESTINATION

Figure 1.1 Your service is a vehicle to get clients from Point A to Point B

a more attractive physique, or a boost in self-confidence. The gym equipment and facilities are merely tools enabling them to reach their fitness goals. They are buying transformation, not access to machines.

This understanding is key to selling and marketing outcomes. It's about reframing your product or service from being a mere commodity to being a solution, a bridge that takes your customer from where they are now to where they want to be. This shift in perspective allows you to better understand your customers, their needs, and the unique value your offering provides.

The heart of outcome-focused marketing and selling is empathy. To sell outcomes, you must first understand the problems and desires of your target market. What keeps them up at night? What are their aspirations? Where do they want to be in six months, a year, or even five years? Once you gain clarity on these points, you can align your product or service as the ideal tool for the transformation they desire.

Take Apple, for example. When they launched the iPod, they didn't market it as a 5GB MP3 player. They sold it as "1000 songs in your pocket." They didn't emphasize the device's technical specifications but focused on the outcome it delivered: an unprecedented level of music portability and accessibility. Apple understood that people weren't just buying an MP3 player; they were buying the ability to have their entire music library at their fingertips, no matter where they were.

Outcomes also form the basis of the value you deliver too.

People are willing to pay more for products and services that deliver desired outcomes more efficiently or effectively. Understanding this can allow you to price your offerings based on the value they provide, not just the cost of the resources involved. The power of an outcome-based approach is undeniable. However, it requires you to shift away from a product-centric mindset. It's about understanding that what you're really selling isn't a product or a service, but a promise—a promise of a better future, a solution to a problem, or a stepping stone towards a goal.

This process starts with really listening to your customers. Understand their needs, their desires, and their fears. Read up on your industry. Check out forums and see what your prospective customers are saying. Use this insight to build your products and services so they address the real needs and wants of the market. You're probably already doing that, but once you understand the outcomes clients want, tailoring your offering to that will make your services easier to market and sell. You need to paint a clear and enticing picture of the future state your customer desires.

Ultimately, selling and marketing outcomes is about positioning your product or service as a vehicle for transformation. It's about showing your customers how you can help them achieve their goals, solve their problems, and improve their situation. In doing so, you're not just selling a product or a service, you're selling a brighter future. And that is a promise worth investing in.

Remember, it's not about the service you provide; it's about the transformation you offer. As you market your services, always highlight how they help your clients achieve their desired future state. (See Table 1.1.)

Table 1.1 Selling transformations for different services.

Service	Transformation Sold
Gym Membership	Enhanced fitness, better health, improved physique
Financial Planner	Wealth growth, financial stability, retirement readiness
Digital Marketing Agency	Increased web traffic, brand recognition, customer engagement
Software as a Service (SaaS)	Improved efficiency, cost savings, streamlined operations
Life Coaching	Improved mindset, achieved goals, enhanced life satisfaction
Home Cleaning Service	Clean, comfortable living space, saved time and effort
Catering Service	Delicious meals for events, hassle-free event planning
Language Learning App	Proficiency in a new language, cultural understanding
Web Development Service	Professional online presence, increased customer trust
Interior Designing Service	Beautiful living space, improved comfort, increased home value
Real Estate Agent	Successful home buying/selling, minimized stress during the process
Graphic Design Service	Visually compelling brand materials, enhanced brand image
Car Rental Service	Convenient transportation, flexibility during travel

Table 1.1 (*Continued*)

Service	Transformation Sold
Meal Delivery Service	Nutritious meals, convenience, saved cooking time
Personal Training	Custom fitness plan, personalized coaching, faster results
Professional Development Courses	Improved skills, career advancement, increased job opportunities

Beach Holidays

Every year, I eagerly anticipate my beach holiday. I'm a sun, sea, and sand kind of guy—the kind who yearns for the warm embrace of a sun-soaked coastline and the comforting rhythm of waves lapping against the shore. I crave the serenity that comes from sitting by a sparkling pool, with a drink in hand, doing little more than soaking in the joy of being away from the daily grind.

However, the week leading up to the holiday is an entirely different story. It's a frantic race against time, a flurry of activity. I'm rushing to tick off everything on my to-do list, working late, and trying to preemptively extinguish potential fires at work. My world becomes a blur of tasks and responsibilities, all in the name of setting myself up for that cherished tranquility on my holiday.

What drives me to dive into this whirlwind of action? What propels me through those long nights and relentless days? Quite simply, it's the anticipation of my beach holiday, the tantalizing image of my future state—reclining on a sun-lounger, the ocean spread out before me, and the world of work a distant memory.

Let's take a moment to consider this in the context of sales and marketing. I see an intriguing parallel between my frenzied preholiday efforts and the way consumers respond to a well-crafted value proposition. Like my anticipation of the beach holiday, a compelling product or service paints a picture of a desirable future state that motivates customers to take action.

Take travel agents, for instance. On the surface, they are selling flights, hotel accommodations, and transfers. These are the tangible products they offer. But if you've ever browsed through a travel brochure or visited a travel website, you'll know that they are selling something much more powerful. They aren't just selling the means of getting from point A to point B. Instead, they're selling the promise of relaxation, adventure, discovery—the chance to create memories that will last a lifetime.

They sell you the scent of the sea, the warmth of the sun on your skin, the taste of exotic cuisine, the sound of a bustling foreign market, and the sight of landscapes you've only ever seen in your dreams. They sell the promise of a new experience, of a break from the mundane, of an opportunity to recharge and rejuvenate.

They are not marketing the hotel's room service or the flight's legroom. Instead, they market the outcome of using their service: the vacation, the break, the escape. They show you pictures of beautiful destinations, enticing you with promises of the joy and relaxation you will experience. It's the vision of these outcomes that propel you to take action, to make a booking, to invest in the promise of a future state that aligns with your desires.

This concept is not exclusive to travel agencies. Regardless of the industry, successful businesses understand that what they are truly selling is not a product or service but an outcome. They recognize that their product or service is merely a vehicle to transport their clients from their current state to a desired future state. It's not the features of the product that hook the customers, but the transformation that the product promises to deliver.

People buy outcomes, not products. They invest in a vision of their future that resonates with them, that promises to bring them closer to their goals, solve their problems, or fulfill their desires. By framing your offerings in terms of outcomes, you can tap into this powerful motivator and encourage your customers to take action. Just as the anticipation of my beach holiday propels me to work harder, so can the promise of a compelling future state drive your customers to engage with your business.

Selling the Dream of a Better Future

So whether you're selling a service, a product, or an experience, it's crucial to remember that you're selling more than just the physical or tangible aspects. You're selling a transformation. You're selling the bridge between where your customer is now and where they aspire to be.

Take an education consulting service as an example. Parents don't hire these consultants simply because they can help with paperwork and applications. They hire them because they promise a future where their child is admitted into a prestigious university, leading to a successful career and a secure life. They aren't buying the service; they're buying the outcome.

The best sales and marketing strategies lean into this understanding. They don't highlight the features or specifications of a product or service. Instead, they emphasize the ways in which their product or service will make the customer's life better, easier, happier, or more fulfilling.

Remember my anticipation for the beach holiday? The most effective marketing strategies harness the power of that anticipation, that vision of a brighter future. They understand that people don't want to buy a quarter-inch drill; they want a quarter-inch hole. They don't want to buy a pair of shoes; they want to feel comfortable and stylish. They don't want to buy a car; they want to experience the freedom and convenience it offers.

This is the art of selling outcomes, of understanding that people are motivated by the promise of a better future. It's about understanding that your product or service is a tool, a means to an end, and not the end itself. So sell the dream, the transformation, the outcome. That's what truly moves people to act.

Whether you're a business owner, a marketer, a salesperson, or an entrepreneur, take this lesson to heart. Don't sell the plane ticket or the hotel room. Sell the sun-kissed beach, the bustling foreign market, the adventure, the relaxation. Sell the destination, not the journey. Because at the end of the day, people don't just buy products or services. They buy outcomes. They buy transformations. They buy dreams. And that's a powerful insight that can transform your sales and marketing strategy.

Clarifying Your Value Proposition

When it comes to marketing outcomes, the type of outcome you choose to focus on will greatly impact the interest you receive from potential clients. The way you market your offering should consider how, when, and where your clients will arrive at their desired destination. These factors determine not only who will be interested but also how much they are willing to invest. Your outcome directly influences your value proposition. Different clients will perceive the value of your outcome differently based on their unique circumstances and preferences.

Think about it: a first-class plane ticket is marketed in a completely different way compared to economy tickets. The outcome of the travel experience, the level of comfort and luxury, and the overall prestige associated with a first-class ticket attract a specific audience. On the other hand, economy tickets appeal to those who prioritize affordability and practicality. A first-class ticket may be chosen for its exclusivity, superior service, and enhanced travel experience.

It appeals to those seeking a luxurious journey and a seamless, stress-free trip. In contrast, an economy ticket caters to individuals who prioritize cost-efficiency and practicality. They may be willing to forgo certain amenities in favor of a budget-friendly option.

The concept of value is intrinsically linked to the outcome you promise. Value is not a fixed measure; it varies based on individual perspectives, needs, and desires. Understanding this distinction is crucial in your marketing strategy.

Moreover, it's important to recognize the difference between needs and wants. Needs are the essential requirements of individuals, the fundamental aspects necessary for survival and functionality. Wants, on the other hand, are aspirational in nature. They represent the desires and dreams individuals hope to fulfill.

When marketing essential outcomes, you are addressing the core needs of your clients. These outcomes provide practical solutions to their pressing problems, offer convenience, or fulfill necessary requirements. On the other hand, marketing aspirational outcomes taps into the desires and dreams of individuals. It's about positioning your product or service to achieve their aspirations and elevate their lives.

Mixing up essential and aspirational outcomes can blur your value proposition. It can lead to confusion among potential clients, as they may not clearly see the specific value you provide. By aligning your marketing efforts with the right outcome, you ensure that your target audience understands the unique value you offer.

Remember, it's crucial to tailor your marketing message to the specific outcome you are promoting. If you're selling essential outcomes, focus on addressing the pain points, challenges, and practical needs of your target audience. Provide them with solutions that meet their immediate requirements. On the other hand, when marketing aspirational outcomes, emphasize the transformation, the fulfillment of desires, and the potential for personal growth and achievement.

By asking yourself key questions about the outcomes you are selling, you can gain clarity and effectively communicate the value you offer. Consider the following questions:

- What is the primary outcome or transformation my product or service delivers?

- How does this outcome align with the needs and desires of my target audience?

- What pain points, challenges, or aspirations does my outcome address?

- What specific benefits and value does my outcome provide to clients?

By answering these questions, you will gain insights into how to define and position your outcome in a way that resonates with your target audience. It will enable you to create compelling marketing messages that clearly communicate the value you provide and attract the right clients who recognize and appreciate the outcome you offer.

The Gaddie Pitch

American author Mark Twain once quipped, "I didn't have time to write a short letter, so I wrote a long one instead." The humor in this statement lies in its paradox, but it also contains an essential truth about communication. Crafting a succinct, impactful message takes a significant amount of thought and consideration. It is this precise art of simplicity that forms the cornerstone of effective marketing.

In an era where information overload is the norm, attention spans are at a premium. Our digital world is a bustling marketplace of ideas, where countless messages clamor for the attention of the audience. Amid this chaos, the simplest message often resonates the loudest. Hence, clarity and brevity should be the guiding principles of your marketing strategy. The outcomes your business offers should be articulated in the most straightforward, relatable, and obvious terms. The faster you can communicate the value you bring to the table, the better positioned you will be in the competitive landscape of your industry.

It's all too easy, especially when you're passionate about your business, to get lost in the intricacies of your offering. To pour every feature, every advantage, every tiny detail into your marketing materials until they're brimming with information. While this may feel comprehensive, it often results in a diluted message that leaves potential customers feeling overwhelmed or confused. Thus, the more we simplify our marketing messages, the easier it is for prospective clients to understand the value we provide and how we can address their needs or pain points.

Many might believe the concept of the elevator pitch, the ability to concisely explain your business within the span of an elevator ride, to be an antiquated concept. But in our current age of bite-sized content and quick-fire digital interactions, it is arguably more relevant than ever. We might not be sharing physical elevators with potential investors or clients, but we are continually competing within their limited timeframes and crowded mental spaces.

In essence, the elevator pitch is not simply about brevity—it's about clarity and focus. It's about distilling your brand, its value proposition, and its unique selling points down to their essence. It forces you to thoroughly understand and articulate the core of what you do and why it matters to your target audience. The better and faster you can communicate this value, the more successful your marketing efforts will be.

Therefore, make Twain's words a mantra for your marketing strategy. Take the time to whittle down your message, honing it until it's as sharp and clear as possible. Prioritize clarity over complexity, succinctness over verbosity, and directness over nuance. Only then will your marketing be able to cut through the noise and make a lasting impression on your audience.

The more specific your outcome, the easier it is to communicate with your prospective clients. Generic or vague outcomes will struggle to punch through the noise and your prospective clients may not see the value of what you do.

When I launched the printing business I described at the beginning of the chapter, I was inadvertently marketing a fast outcome and a cheap outcome. As a result, I attracted curiosity from prospects who wanted a cheap price and a quick turnaround.

Anthony Gaddie, an Australian marketing maverick, devised an ingenious yet simple marketing formula known as the Gaddie Pitch. Revered within the industry for its effectiveness, this tool can aid in concisely communicating your value proposition to your target audience.

You know how . . . (Target Audience) + (State the Problem)
What we do is (Outcome) + (Feelings)

The Gaddie Pitch hinges on a simple structure, consisting of four essential elements:

1. **Target Audience:** This refers to whom your service or product is intended, the segment of the population that stands to benefit the most from what you have to offer.

2. **Pain/Problem:** This component highlights the primary issue or challenge that your product or service is designed to address. It's the crux of your audience's pain points that you can alleviate.

3. **Outcome/Result:** This part focuses on the transformation that your service or product offers—the tangible or intangible benefits or changes that occur as a result of using your product or engaging your services.

4. **Feelings:** This element addresses the emotional response or the feeling that customers get from experiencing the outcome/result. It can be a sense of satisfaction, relief, happiness, or any other positive emotion that is elicited from achieving the desired outcome.

Now that we've clarified the key elements, let's delve deeper into the Gaddie Pitch by breaking down its formula, using an example from my own business.

You know how solopreneurs and small business owners struggle to market and sell themselves?

What I do is give them straightforward strategies they can implement, so they feel confident to act.

Just recently, I shared a simple social media commenting strategy with a solopreneur who sells her expertise to startups. She implemented the strategy and picked up a £40k client.

The formula begins with the phrase "You know how . . ." followed by your target audience and the problem they typically face. This part of the pitch is crafted to resonate with your prospective customers, helping them feel understood and validating their struggles. For example, "You know how small business owners often struggle with marketing their services effectively?"

Next comes the transformation your business offers. This is the outcome/result coupled with the feeling it elicits. This part is crucial because it's where you make your value proposition clear, demonstrating how your offering improves your customers' lives or

15

businesses. For instance, "What we do is provide simple, actionable marketing strategies that not only boost their visibility but also give them a sense of confidence and control over their business growth."

In its entirety, the pitch reads: "You know how small business owners often struggle with marketing their services effectively? What we do is provide simple, actionable marketing strategies that not only boost their visibility but also give them a sense of confidence and control over their business growth."

The simplicity and effectiveness of the Gaddie Pitch lie in its customer-centric approach. It starts with the customers' pain points, offers a solution, and then concludes with the positive feelings evoked by that solution. This format resonates with the target audience, ensuring that your value proposition is communicated effectively.

A simple framework like the Gaddie Pitch can quickly help people see your value. It creates curiosity about what you do and how you do it, which is key to getting leads and inquiries.

Having a simple and quick way to explain your value can massively improve your marketing success. Prospects don't give you the benefit of the doubt. They look and, if it interests them, they keep reading. If it isn't relevant, they move on. You may have seconds to get their attention and interest.

That's why the Gaddie Pitch is so powerful. Just thinking about it in the context of a 30-second explainer will give you so much clarity and focus. From that focus you can repurpose that statement into visuals, copy, and campaigns.

Transforming Curiosity into Sales

Having clear outcomes from your services and leveraging them in your marketing is critical to driving leads and inquiries. In today's saturated market, the secret to captivating your audience, generating leads, and driving sales inquiries lies not in the services or products you offer. Instead, it's the specific outcomes your audience can achieve using your offerings that spark curiosity and initiate the buying journey.

When we are solopreneurs or small business owners, our products or services are the vehicles that drive customers toward their desired outcomes. But the customer's journey isn't about the vehicle; it's about the destination. It's not about the features of your product or service. It's about the transformation, the tangible results, the problem solved, or the improved situation your offering promises.

Implementing outcome-focused marketing means shifting your narrative to spotlight the benefits customers will experience, the problems they will solve, and the improved state they will achieve. This approach inherently sparks curiosity, as it aligns with the customer's core motivations, desires, and needs.

For instance, a digital marketing agency doesn't merely sell SEO services. They sell increased website traffic, higher search engine rankings, and ultimately more customers. A fitness coach doesn't simply offer personal training sessions. They sell improved health, increased energy, and body transformations. By marketing these outcomes, they tap into the heart of their customers' aspirations, triggering curiosity to learn more about how these desirable results can be achieved.

Moreover, when you specify potential outcomes, you facilitate your prospects' visualization of their future state—a powerful catalyst for curiosity. When prospects can imagine the impact your offerings could have on their lives or businesses, it naturally prompts them to seek more information, leading to increased leads and sales inquiries.

Curiosity, as an innate human instinct, is an essential ingredient in the recipe for marketing success. When effectively ignited, it serves as the gateway to engagement, leads, and sales.

The psychology behind this is simple. Curiosity triggers a gap in our knowledge—a gap we are compelled to fill. When your marketing sparks curiosity about potential outcomes, it nudges prospects to bridge that knowledge gap by reaching out, initiating contact, or making an inquiry. This interaction marks the beginning of the sales funnel, transitioning prospects from passive observers to active leads.

Curiosity, however, is only the initial spark. Your role as a business owner is to fan that spark into a flame, transforming curiosity into tangible sales. This is achieved through effective follow-up communication, demonstrations of value, and maintaining focus on the outcome throughout the sales process.

Continuously emphasize how your offering can deliver the outcomes your prospects desire. Use testimonials, case studies, and real-life examples to showcase past success stories, enabling prospects to see your product or service's potential. Maintain the focus on outcomes during sales conversations, resisting the urge to dive too deep into the features or technical aspects of your offering.

Pivoting your marketing strategy to highlight specific outcomes, rather than the features of your product or service, is a powerful way to spark curiosity in your potential customers. This curiosity is the key to generating leads and driving sales inquiries, marking the beginning of a fruitful customer journey. By maintaining a steady focus on outcomes throughout this journey, you can effectively transform curiosity into sales, creating satisfied customers and growing your business. Remember, you change your world by selling outcomes. Each outcome achieved for a customer brings them closer to their goals and aspirations, making a positive impact on their lives. By embracing the mindset of selling outcomes, you not only drive your own business success but also contribute to the success and transformation of your customers. So let your marketing be driven by the power of outcomes, ignite curiosity, and watch as your business flourishes, one satisfied customer at a time.

Chapter 2

Knowing Your Most Valuable Clients

In the world of business, not all clients are created equal. Some clients bring more value, satisfaction, and growth opportunities to your business than others. These are your Most Valuable Clients (MVCs)—the dream clients you should prioritize and focus on. In this explainer, we will dive into what MVCs are and why they are crucial for your business, and provide examples of why focusing on them can lead to greater success.

MVCs are a subset of your total addressable market that aligns perfectly with your business. They are the clients who truly understand and appreciate the value you offer. MVCs are not just customers who generate higher revenue; they are the ones who make your work enjoyable, fulfilling, and profitable. These clients are the perfect fit for your business, and they bring numerous benefits beyond financial gains.

MVCs are clients you find easy to work with. There is a natural synergy between your skills and expertise and their needs and expectations. This alignment fosters smoother communication, mutual understanding, and a more enjoyable collaboration process.

By focusing on MVCs, you can deliver exceptional value that precisely meets their needs. This leads to higher levels of customer satisfaction, because you can tailor your products or services to exceed their expectations. Satisfied MVCs become loyal advocates who refer new business to you.

MVCs are often willing to pay a premium for your offerings because they recognize and appreciate the unique value you bring. This higher willingness to invest translates into increased profitability for your business. By focusing on MVCs, you can create pricing strategies that reflect the value you provide and optimize your profitability.

By understanding the specific needs and preferences of your MVCs, you gain valuable insights that can help you refine and optimize your offerings. With a clear focus on serving these dream clients, you can develop products or services that precisely address their pain points and deliver the outcomes they desire.

For many businesses, targeting their entire market can be an expensive and ineffective approach. It requires significant resources, in terms of both time and money, to reach a wide audience. However, most businesses, especially small businesses, don't need hundreds or even thousands of clients to thrive. In fact, they can achieve their goals with just a handful of new clients each month. This is where the concept of focusing on MVCs becomes highly valuable.

Think about it for a moment. Let's say you only need three or four new clients each month to meet your revenue targets. In this scenario, it makes perfect sense to prioritize your efforts and resources on attracting and serving your dream clients. These are the clients who align closely with your ideal customer profile, appreciate the value you offer, and are willing to pay for it.

When you narrow your focus to a specific subset of your target market, you can fine-tune your marketing strategies and messaging to resonate more effectively with that group. Rather than casting a wide net and hoping to catch any potential client, you can craft tailored marketing campaigns that address the specific needs, pain points, and desires of your MVCs. This targeted approach allows you to cut through the noise and connect more meaningfully with the people who are most likely to convert into loyal customers. (See Table 2.1.)

Table 2.1 How your MVCs differ from your entire market.

Your Entire Market	Most Valuable Clients
Broad and generalized target audience	Specific subset of the target market
Demographics and basic characteristics	Deep understanding of their needs, pain points, and desires
One-size-fits-all marketing approach	Tailored marketing strategies and messaging
Lower conversion rates	Higher conversion rates due to targeted approach
More time and resources required	Efficient use of resources and time with targeted efforts
Less clarity on ideal client profile	Clear identification of ideal client profile
Inconsistent messaging and branding	Consistent messaging and branding aligned with MVCs
Difficulty in standing out from competitors	Unique value proposition tailored to MVCs
Vague understanding of client motivations	In-depth knowledge of client motivations and desires
Lower customer loyalty and repeat business	Stronger customer loyalty and repeat business

Instead of spreading yourself too thin trying to cater to a broad audience, you can concentrate your efforts on reaching and engaging with the individuals or businesses that hold the greatest potential. This allows you to make the most of your time, energy, and budget, focusing on activities that generate the highest return on investment.

Making Marketing Easier

When you have a clear understanding of who your dream clients are, what motivates them, and how your offerings can address their needs, it becomes easier to create compelling marketing messages and develop targeted campaigns. You can speak directly to the pain points and aspirations of your MVCs, demonstrating your deep understanding of their unique challenges and desires.

Identifying your MVCs is just the beginning. To maintain a competitive edge and continue to attract dream clients, it's crucial to continuously analyze and adapt your approach. Market dynamics change, client needs evolve, and new opportunities arise. Regularly reassess your MVCs, refine your offerings, and ensure you remain aligned with their evolving needs and desires.

Focusing on your MVCs offers numerous benefits that can drive your business growth and success. Let's reframe the previous points into the benefits of having a defined MVC:

- **Clarity and Direction:** Having a defined MVC provides clarity and direction for your marketing efforts. It allows you to identify and understand your ideal clients, enabling you to create focused strategies and targeted messaging that resonate with them. This clarity helps you streamline your marketing activities and ensures a more efficient use of resources.

- **Efficient Resource Allocation:** By concentrating your efforts on your MVCs, you can allocate your resources more efficiently. Instead of spreading yourself thin across a broad customer base, you can invest your time, energy, and budget into channels and strategies that directly reach and engage your ideal clients. This targeted approach maximizes your return on investment and improves overall marketing effectiveness.

- **Strong Brand Identity:** Focusing on your MVCs allows you to build a strong brand identity that aligns with their needs and preferences. By understanding your ideal clients' values, pain points, and desired outcomes, you can craft a brand message that resonates deeply with them. This alignment fosters brand loyalty, recognition, and differentiation from competitors.

- **Personalization and Customization:** A defined MVC enables you to deliver personalized and customized solutions. By understanding the specific needs, preferences, and goals of your MVCs, you can tailor your offerings to address their unique challenges. This level of personalization enhances customer satisfaction, builds trust, and strengthens long-term relationships.

- **Growth Opportunities:** Focusing on your MVCs helps you identify and seize growth opportunities within specific segments or industries. By deepening your understanding of your ideal clients, their pain points, and their industry dynamics, you can position yourself as an expert and cater to their specialized needs. This specialization opens doors to new markets, referrals, and partnerships, fueling your business growth.

- **Differentiation from Competitors:** Having a defined MVC allows you to differentiate yourself from competitors in a crowded marketplace. By understanding your ideal clients' motivations and desires, you can emphasize the unique value and benefits you offer. This differentiation helps you stand out, attract attention, and position your business as the preferred choice for your target audience.

- **Consistent Customer Experience:** Focusing on your MVCs enables you to consistently deliver a remarkable customer experience. By understanding their expectations and preferences, you can tailor your interactions, communication, and service delivery to meet and exceed their needs. Consistency in customer experience builds loyalty, enhances reputation, and generates positive word-of-mouth referrals.

Having a defined MVC brings clarity, efficiency, and effectiveness to your marketing efforts. It helps you build a strong brand, deliver personalized solutions, identify growth opportunities, differentiate from competitors, and create exceptional customer experiences. By focusing on your MVCs, you position your business for long-term success and sustainable growth.

Identifying Your Most Valuable Clients

To identify your Most Valuable Clients (MVCs), it's important to have a clear understanding of their characteristics, needs, and preferences.

Asking the right questions can provide valuable insights that help you narrow down your target audience and tailor your marketing efforts accordingly.

Here are 20 questions to guide you in identifying your MVCs. By reflecting on these questions and analyzing the patterns in your responses, you can gain clarity on who your ideal clients are and how to best serve them. This knowledge will empower you to focus your resources on attracting and retaining the clients who bring the most value to your business.

1. Who are your current best clients, the ones you enjoy working with the most?

2. What specific industries or sectors do your ideal clients belong to?

3. What is the size of the company or organization that aligns best with your expertise?

4. Are your MVCs primarily individuals or businesses?

5. Where are your MVCs located geographically?

6. What are the common challenges or pain points that your MVCs face?

7. What are the specific goals or outcomes that your MVCs are seeking to achieve?

8. Do your MVCs have a certain level of budget or financial resources to invest in your services?

9. What are the common values or beliefs that your MVCs share?

10. Are there any demographic characteristics that your MVCs have in common (age, gender, education, etc.)?

11. Do your MVCs have any specific psychographic traits or behaviors that differentiate them from other clients?

12. Are your MVCs decision-makers within their organizations or do they require approval from higher-ups?

13. Do your MVCs prioritize quality, speed, cost-effectiveness, or other factors in their decision-making?

14. Are your MVCs seeking long-term partnerships or are they more focused on short-term projects?

15. Are your MVCs actively searching for solutions to their challenges, or do they need to be convinced of the value?

16. Do your MVCs have any specific preferences or requirements when it comes to communication and collaboration?

17. Are your MVCs open to innovation and trying new approaches, or do they prefer traditional methods?

18. Are there any specific events, conferences, or industry associations that your MVCs actively engage with?

19. Have your MVCs expressed dissatisfaction with existing service providers or solutions in the market?

20. Have your MVCs provided positive testimonials or referrals that indicate their satisfaction with your services?

Creating a Buyer Persona

Once you've started to nail down who your MVC is, it's time to lock it down into a buyer persona. A buyer persona is a fictional representation of your ideal customer based on market research and data about your existing customers. It is a detailed profile that helps you understand the demographics, behaviors, motivations, and preferences of your target audience. A buyer persona goes beyond simple demographics and delves into the psychology and specific characteristics of your customers.

Creating a buyer persona involves collecting information about your customers through various methods such as surveys, interviews, and data analysis. This information helps you develop a comprehensive understanding of your customers' needs, challenges, goals, and purchasing behaviors. By humanizing your target audience, a buyer persona allows you to better empathize with them and create marketing strategies that resonate with their unique needs and desires.

A buyer persona typically includes details such as age, gender, job title, income level, education, and location. It also goes deeper by capturing information about their interests, motivations, pain points, preferred communication channels, and purchasing habits. The persona is often given a name and a visual representation to make it more relatable and memorable.

Having well-defined buyer personas helps you make informed decisions about product development, marketing campaigns, and customer service. It allows you to tailor your messaging, content, and offerings to effectively engage and connect with your target audience.

By understanding your customers on a deeper level, you can deliver a personalized experience that addresses their specific needs and ultimately drives more successful business outcomes.

Giving your MVC a persona helps bring them to life in your marketing campaigns and outreach activity. It helps you talk to exactly the right people, as described in the following example.

Financial Fred

A buyer persona for senior executives in financial services would be a detailed profile that represents the key characteristics, preferences, and motivations of this specific target audience. We create a written persona, so that we can craft our content, slogans, and marketing campaigns and never lose sight of who these are for. It's an anchor for our marketing and sales activity.

It's easy to say, "I know who my clients are" but it is much easier to drift off and start creating random marketing that doesn't speak to your MVCs.

Let's call our buyer persona Financial Executive Fred. Here's a practical explanation of what Financial Executive Fred might look like:

> Financial Executive Fred is a 50-year-old senior executive with extensive experience in the financial services industry. He holds a high-level position in a large financial institution and has a strong background in investment management. He is typically a decision-maker or influencer within his organization when it comes to financial solutions and services.
>
> Fred's professional goals revolve around achieving strategic growth, maximizing profitability, and mitigating risks for his company. He is constantly seeking innovative ways to optimize financial performance and stay ahead in

a highly competitive industry. Fred values expertise, credibility, and proven track records when considering business partnerships or investment opportunities.

In terms of preferences, Fred stays informed about industry trends through reputable financial publications, professional networks, and industry conferences. He appreciates data-driven insights and comprehensive reports that can help him make informed decisions. Fred prefers efficient and streamlined communication channels, such as email or scheduled meetings, given his busy schedule.

When it comes to challenges, Fred may face pressure to adapt to changing regulations, technological advancements, and evolving customer expectations. He is always on the lookout for solutions that can address these challenges while improving operational efficiency and maintaining compliance.

Financial Executive Fred's buyer persona helps financial services providers understand his needs and tailor their offerings accordingly. For example, a company targeting senior executives like Fred may emphasize their experience and expertise in providing strategic financial solutions, showcasing case studies that demonstrate successful outcomes. They might also highlight their commitment to compliance and the ability to navigate complex regulatory environments.

Understanding Financial Executive Fred's buyer persona enables a business to craft targeted marketing messages, create relevant content, and develop solutions that align with his unique requirements. By speaking directly to the pain points, goals, and preferences of senior executives in financial services, I could position myself as a trusted partner and engage buyers like Fred in a more relevant way.

What other advantages does a persona give me?

Well, once I have a persona identified, I can use that to determine which marketing and sales channels will work the best. Is it necessary to invest time on TikTok to market my business to a 50-plus financial services executive? Should I be posting stories on Instagram? Should I invest in advertising in industry magazines?

Not every channel is needed because my persona is Fred and the likelihood of being able to successfully engage Fred on TikTok may not be the best use of my time and energy.

A buyer persona brings clarity to your marketing and anchors your message, so you never lose sight of who your marketing is for.

Chapter 3

Creating Your Offer

I'll be honest with you. I had a ridiculous fear—a fear that held me back from attracting clients and growing my business. It was the fear of focus. I had this notion that if I narrowed down my offering too much, I would miss out on potential business. I was afraid that by being too specific, I would turn people away. Little did I know that this fear was hindering my success and preventing me from creating compelling offers for my clients.

My fear of focus kept me from raising awareness about the specific ways I could help my clients. Instead of having a clear and defined package that people could easily understand and inquire about, I kept things vague and ambiguous. I thought that by not being too specific, I would leave room for any potential opportunity. But the truth is, my lack of focus made it difficult for prospective clients to see how I could truly assist them. It created confusion rather than curiosity.

Then I had a realization. I discovered that not having a clear offer was hindering my business growth. I realized that prospective clients needed something tangible to latch onto. They wanted a clear package that addressed their specific needs and provided a defined outcome and process. As soon as I started creating clear offers for my prospective clients, something amazing happened: the number of inquiries increased.

So what do I mean by an offer? An offer is more than just a product or service. It's a well-defined package that prospective clients can purchase, with a clear outcome and a step-by-step process. It provides a solution to their specific problem or helps them achieve a desired result. An offer takes the abstract and makes it concrete. It gives your clients something to grasp onto and understand. It shows them exactly how you can help and why they should choose you.

When you have clear offers, something magical happens. Your MVCs no longer have to guess or wonder about what you can do for them. They can see it right in front of them. Clear offers create a sense of confidence and trust. They show that you understand your clients' needs and have a proven method to address them. This clarity not only attracts more inquiries, but it also helps to qualify your leads. Those who resonate with your offer are more likely to become your ideal clients.

I know that the fear of focus can be paralyzing. You might worry that by narrowing down your offering, you're limiting your opportunities. But here's the truth: by being focused, you're opening up a world of possibilities. By defining your offer and clearly communicating its value, you become a magnet for the right clients. You attract those who are specifically looking for what you have to offer. And by focusing on your strengths and expertise, you position yourself as an authority in your field.

Your offer is simply how you choose to package your services. Aligning your service to your MVCs, their desired outcome, with your process and price to achieve it, you can show your value. (See Figure 3.1.)

The outcome and price help your MVCs determine whether it is worth purchasing. How you tailor it for your MVCs and your process supports the client's belief your offer is relevant to them. Now let's examine more closely these four steps of creating your offer, and then we'll look at what you can do to reduce the perceived risk your offer entails.

- Most Valuable Clients
- Specific Outcome (Value)
- Your Process to Achieve it
- Your Price (Cost)

Figure 3.1   Creating Your Offer

Step 1: Identifying Your Most Valuable Clients (MVCs)

Identifying your most valuable clients (MVCs) is the first crucial step in constructing a compelling offer. These are the clients who bring the most value to your business, appreciate your unique value proposition, and are willing to invest in your services. By focusing on your MVCs, you can tailor your marketing efforts and offerings to specifically cater to their needs and desires, increasing your chances of attracting and retaining high-value clients.

Here are some tips to help you identify your MVCs:

1. Analyze your existing client base:
    - Look for common characteristics among your most satisfied and profitable clients.
    - Identify patterns related to industry, demographics, psychographics, and purchasing behavior.
    - Consider clients who have referred others to your business or have shown long-term loyalty.

2. Conduct market research:

- Use surveys, interviews, or customer feedback sessions to gain insights into client preferences and pain points.
- Seek feedback on what aspects of your product or service have provided the most value to clients.
- Look for trends and recurring themes that indicate common needs or desires among your clients.

3. Segment your client base:

- Divide your clients into groups based on similarities in their needs, behaviors, or characteristics.
- Develop buyer personas that represent the ideal traits of your MVCs.
- Consider factors such as industry, company size, job title, geographic location, or specific pain points.

4. Look for profitability indicators:

- Evaluate the financial impact of each client by analyzing metrics such as lifetime value, repeat purchases, or average transaction size.
- Identify clients who have generated the highest revenue or provided the most significant return on investment.

5. Seek referrals and testimonials:

- Reach out to satisfied clients and ask for referrals to others who may benefit from your offerings.
- Request testimonials or case studies that highlight the positive outcomes achieved by working with your business.
- Use these referrals and testimonials to identify patterns among your most valuable clients.

6. Monitor customer engagement and satisfaction:

- Pay attention to clients who actively engage with your content, attend your events, or participate in your loyalty programs.

- Measure customer satisfaction through surveys or Net Promoter Score (NPS) assessments.

- Identify clients who consistently provide positive feedback and have a strong affinity for your brand.

Step 2: Defining the Desired Outcome

Once you have identified your most valuable clients (MVCs), the next step in constructing your offer is to define the desired outcome. The desired outcome is the specific result or transformation that your MVCs are seeking when they engage with your product or service. By understanding and articulating this outcome, you can align your offer with their goals and position yourself as the solution to their needs.

1. Listen to your MVCs:

- Engage in conversations with your MVCs to understand their aspirations, challenges, and desired outcomes.

- Ask open-ended questions to encourage them to share their goals and expectations.

- Pay attention to their language, emotions, and motivations to gain deeper insights into what they truly desire.

2. Conduct market research:

- Study your target market and industry to identify common goals and desires among your MVCs.

- Analyze industry trends, customer feedback, and competitor offerings to gain a comprehensive understanding of the desired outcomes.

3. Use empathy and put yourself in their shoes:

- Imagine the perspective of your MVCs and consider what they truly want to achieve.

- Understand the emotions, pain points, and challenges they may face in reaching their desired outcome.

- Align your messaging and offer to address their needs and provide a clear path to their desired result.

4. Focus on specific and tangible outcomes:

- Clearly define the specific result or transformation that your MVCs can expect from your product or service.

- Use concrete and measurable terms to describe the outcome, such as increased revenue, improved efficiency, enhanced well-being, or expanded market reach.

- Avoid vague or ambiguous language that may create confusion or uncertainty about the value you provide.

5. Prioritize high-impact outcomes:

- Identify the outcomes that have the most significant impact on your MVCs' lives or businesses.

- Understand which outcomes are the most critical to their success and well-being.

- Prioritize these high-impact outcomes in your offer and emphasize the value they deliver.

6. Consider both short-term and long-term outcomes:

- Address immediate needs and provide solutions that yield quick wins for your MVCs.

- Also, consider the long-term goals and aspirations of your MVCs, and position your offer as a vehicle for sustained growth and success.

Step 3: Developing the Process

Once you have identified your most valuable clients (MVCs) and defined the desired outcome, the next step in constructing your offer is to develop a clear and effective process. The process outlines the steps, methods, and actions you will take to help your MVCs achieve the desired outcome. It provides a roadmap that brings confidence in your MVCs, demonstrating that you have a structured approach to deliver the results they seek.

Your outcome is supported by your process. Anyone can promise an outcome, but your process is designed to create the milestones to achieving that outcome. It provides substance to your outcome.

Here are some tips to help you develop an effective process for your offer:

1. Identify key milestones:
   - Break down the journey to the desired outcome into key milestones or stages.
   - Define the significant steps that your MVCs need to take to progress towards their goal.
   - Make sure each milestone is clear, actionable, and aligned with the overall desired outcome.
2. Communicate the process clearly:
   - Clearly outline the steps involved in your process, using language that is easy for your MVCs to understand.

- Avoid jargon or technical terms that may confuse or overwhelm your MVCs.

- Use visual aids such as flow charts or diagrams to visually represent the process and make it more accessible.

3. Highlight the value of each step:

- Clearly explain the value and benefits that each step in the process brings to your MVCs.

- Show how each step contributes to their progress towards the desired outcome.

- Emphasize how your expertise and unique approach make each step valuable and impactful.

4. Customize the process:

- Tailor the process to the specific needs and preferences of your MVCs.

- Consider their unique circumstances, goals, and challenges when designing the process.

- Personalize the process to create a sense of individualized attention and care.

5. Be transparent about timeframes:

- Clearly communicate the estimated timeframes for each step in the process.

- Be realistic and honest about the time it may take to achieve the desired outcome.

- Manage expectations by setting realistic timelines and addressing potential delays or challenges.

6. Offer flexibility and adaptability:

- Recognize that every MVC may have unique requirements or circumstances.

- Build flexibility into your process to accommodate different needs or preferences.

- Be open to adjusting the process based on individual situations while maintaining the overall goal.

Step 4: Determining the Price

The fourth step in constructing your offer is to determine the price. Pricing plays a crucial role in the perceived value of your offer and directly impacts the decision-making process of your potential clients. When determining the price, it's important to consider the value you deliver, the market dynamics, and the financial goals of your business.

Pricing is a funny thing. Traditionally people would price based on the cost, plus a margin. When I worked with a large print business in the late 2000s, they were making a 20% margin on every sale. But you don't have to price that way; you can price based on the value of the outcome. For example, is a luxury vehicle really priced on the cost of the car itself, or is it priced based on the brand and prestige it unlocks for customers? The average price of a Rolls Royce is around $540,000, but is that representative of its cost? While the profit margins on vehicles aren't public, it is estimated they make up to 40% margin on every vehicle. That's over $200,000 profit per vehicle.

Pricing on value is about aligning your price to the value it unlocks for customers. Low pricing can be an obstacle to purchasing. As human beings we have an inbuilt understanding that valuable things cost money. When we see high value and a low price, we suspect it may not be as good as it promises to be. We are innately skeptical of low prices with high returns.

Most of our individual experience has proven this skepticism correct, because most of the easy wins or low-cost deals have turned out to be scams or have not lived up to expectations.

Here are some key considerations and tips for determining the price of your offer:

1. **Assess the value delivered:**

   - Evaluate the outcomes, benefits, and results your offer provides to your MVCs.

   - Consider the impact and transformation that your service brings to their lives or businesses.

   - Quantify the value delivered in terms of time saved, increased revenue, improved efficiency, or emotional well-being.

2. **Understand your market:**

   - Research and analyze the market to gain insights into the pricing landscape for similar offers.

   - Determine the price range that aligns with the perceived value and quality of your offer.

   - Consider the pricing strategies used by competitors and how you can differentiate your offer.

3. **Position your offer:**

   - Position your offer as a premium solution by highlighting the unique value and benefits it provides.

   - Differentiate yourself from competitors by emphasizing the specific advantages of your offer.

   - Assess the preferences and purchasing behavior of your MVCs to choose the most suitable pricing structure.

4. **Consider costs and expenses:**

   - Evaluate the costs associated with delivering your offer, including materials, resources, and time.

- Factor in any overhead costs, operational expenses, or ongoing maintenance required.

- Ensure that the price covers your expenses while allowing for a reasonable profit margin.

5. Offer pricing options:

- Provide pricing options that cater to different budgets and needs.

- Consider offering tiered packages or add-on services to allow for customization and flexibility.

- Present the pricing options clearly and transparently to facilitate decision-making.

Reducing the Risk in Your Offer

When clients assess the value of a service, they often rely on a mental equation that factors in the importance and impact of the outcome compared to the price. This equation helps them determine the worthiness of the investment based on their individual needs and priorities. For example, an ambitious manager in a large corporate business who is moving up to a more senior role involving lots of million-dollar sales pitch presentations will value self-confidence coaching more than a small business owner who needs to increase their confidence for business networking.

The stakes are higher and so the value of the outcome is higher—this means they expect to pay more for a more valuable outcome.

When clients evaluate the value of a service, they often engage in a mental equation that allows them to compare the anticipated outcomes against the associated price. This equation is an internal assessment that helps them determine the worthiness of the investment based on their unique needs, priorities, and perceived value.

The mental equation involves several considerations. First, clients evaluate the importance of the desired outcome in their lives. They reflect on how significant and impactful achieving that outcome would be for them personally or professionally. This importance can stem from various factors, such as achieving a long-term goal, overcoming a challenge, or fulfilling a deep-seated desire. Clients inherently assign value to the outcome based on the level of importance they attribute to it.

Second, clients assess the potential benefits they expect to derive from the service. They consider how the outcome will positively affect their lives, addressing specific pain points or fulfilling specific needs. This evaluation encompasses both tangible and intangible benefits. Tangible benefits may include increased efficiency, cost savings, or improved performance. Intangible benefits may include enhanced well-being, increased confidence, or a sense of fulfillment. Clients weigh these benefits against the price to determine if the value proposition aligns with their expectations.

Furthermore, clients consider the uniqueness and exclusivity of the service. They consider whether the offering is differentiated from competitors or readily available alternatives. Clients recognize that specialized expertise, a unique approach, or a tailored solution often come at a higher price. The perception of exclusivity can influence the perceived value and, consequently, the willingness to pay.

Clients also factor in their past experiences and knowledge. They draw upon their own history of investing in similar services or products, considering the outcomes they obtained in relation to the price paid. Positive experiences and successful outcomes tend to reinforce the belief that investing in a particular service is worthwhile, while negative experiences may raise skepticism or hesitation.

The perceived risk associated with the investment is another element of the mental equation. Clients assess the potential downside or loss if the service fails to deliver the anticipated outcome. This evaluation is crucial because it affects the perceived value of the service. Providers who effectively mitigate risks, offer guarantees, or provide testimonials and case studies to demonstrate reliability and success can help alleviate these concerns and increase the perceived value.

Factors like how long they have been aware of you, how comfortable you are in conversation, and how well you engage all play a part in increasing or decreasing the risk of investing. One of the big keys in reducing the risk for the client is having a clearly defined process as part of your offer. This way clients can see how you can help them achieve the promised outcome.

Having a defined process to achieve a desired outcome for a client can significantly help reduce the perceived risk of buying your service. When potential clients are considering investing in your service, they often experience a certain level of uncertainty and concern about the outcome they will receive. By outlining a clear and structured process, you can alleviate their fears, build trust, and increase their confidence in your ability to deliver the desired results.

One of the primary reasons why a defined process reduces perceived risk is that it provides transparency and clarity. Clients want to know what to expect when they engage your services. They want reassurance that you have a systematic approach in place to address their needs and guide them towards the desired outcome. By articulating and communicating your process, you demonstrate that you have a well-thought-out methodology to achieve results.

The defined process serves as a roadmap that outlines the steps, actions, and milestones involved in working with a client. It sets clear expectations and establishes a sense of structure. This helps clients feel more at ease as they can visualize the journey and understand the path they will be taking towards their desired outcome. When clients have a clear understanding of the process, they are more likely to trust in your expertise and commit to working with you.

Moreover, a defined process provides reassurance by highlighting your experience and expertise in the field. When you showcase a structured approach, it demonstrates that you have successfully guided previous clients through similar journeys. This builds confidence in your abilities and reduces the perceived risk associated with trying an unknown service provider. Clients feel more comfortable knowing that you have a proven track record and a system in place to address their specific needs.

The process also helps manage expectations. When clients have a clear understanding of what will happen at each stage of the process, they are less likely to have unrealistic or misguided expectations. This reduces the risk of disappointment or dissatisfaction. By openly communicating the steps involved, potential clients can assess whether the process aligns with their own timeline, commitments, and objectives. They can make an informed decision based on their level of readiness and their confidence in your ability to deliver the desired outcome within their desired timeframe.

If I present you with a great deal, sure you'll be curious, but the next phase of that interest is to scratch the surface and see if it is legit or too good to be true. When clients see that you have a structured approach in place, they gain confidence in the deliverability of the outcome. They feel more confident that you can get them to the desired outcome.

A structured process provides a sense of professionalism and credibility. Clients are more likely to trust and value your service if you show them a systematic approach. It conveys that you take your work seriously and are committed to providing a high level of service. This professionalism gives prospective clients confidence, making them more willing to invest.

Clients evaluate the overall fit between their needs, expectations, and the offering. They consider how well the service aligns with their specific goals, preferences, and desired outcomes. Clients seek assurance that the service provider understands their circumstances and can deliver the desired results. The perceived fit between the service and their individual needs further influences the perceived value. For example, if I have a defined outcome and process and it doesn't fit my client's way of working, they may not appreciate the value as much as another where my process fits like a glove for what they need. That changes the value. This is why having MVCs and documenting your buyer persona can make your offer so powerful and reduce the friction in the sales process. It's like your offer is perfect for them.

The mental equation clients use to calculate the value versus price is not a precise formula but rather a subjective evaluation based on their own perspective and circumstances. It is influenced by their individual motivations, priorities, and beliefs. The more you understand your MVCs, the more you can address their concerns, highlight the unique benefits, and convey the value they will receive. It strengthens their perception of the service's worth and increases their confidence in the investment.

Remember that the mental equation is dynamic and can vary from client to client. By engaging in open communication, actively listening to their needs, and customizing your offerings to match their unique requirements, you can enhance the perceived value and build stronger relationships with your clients.

Chapter 4

Building Your Message to the World

You've defined your MVC, you have a clear offer for them, and now it's time to clarify your message. This is where the power of personal branding and consistency can work in your favor.

Your message for the world needs to be clear, compelling, concise, and consistent. However—and wherever you use it—it needs to convey the value, benefits, and unique selling proposition you offer.

The purpose of a marketing message is to clearly articulate the value proposition of your product or service, highlighting its unique features, benefits, and advantages over competitors. It should answer the fundamental question of "Why should customers choose you?" by addressing their pain points, needs, and desires.

Your message should capture the key elements of your offering and effectively communicate it to your target audience. It is designed to grab attention, generate interest, and ultimately persuade your target customers to act.

To create an impactful marketing message, it is essential to understand your MVCs and tailor your message specifically to their preferences, challenges, and aspirations. By doing so, you can speak directly to their needs and establish a connection that resonates with them. You become more relevant to the people who really matter, the ones you want to work with.

A well-crafted marketing message should be clear, concise, and easy enough for a six-year-old to understand. It should be communicated in a language that your target audience can relate to, avoiding jargon or technical terms that may confuse or alienate them. The message should be persuasive, conveying the benefits and outcomes that customers can expect from using your product or service.

One of the most useful tools is to adapt your Gaddie pitch we discussed in Chapter 1 into a big promise statement.

The Big Promise

A big promise is a compelling commitment or assurance made to potential customers about the transformation or results they can expect to achieve by using a product or service. It is a bold and persuasive statement that captures the ultimate benefit or outcome that customers can anticipate.

The essence of a big promise is to communicate a significant positive change or solution to a problem that resonates with the target audience. It goes beyond the features and functionalities of the product or service and focuses on the impact it will have on the customers' lives, businesses, or well-being.

A big promise serves as a persuasive tool to capture attention, generate interest, and differentiate your offering from competitors. It creates an emotional connection and inspires MVCs to envision a better future by leveraging your product or service.

Every business, regardless of its size or industry, has a form of big promise that communicates the value, benefits, or outcomes it offers to its customers. A big promise represents the core proposition of a business and encapsulates the transformation or results customers can expect by engaging with the brand.

Let's explore some examples of well-known brands and their big promises:

- **Apple, "Think Different":** Apple's big promise revolves around challenging the status quo, encouraging creativity, and providing innovative technology that empowers individuals to think differently and accomplish extraordinary things.

- **Nike, "Just Do It":** Nike's big promise inspires customers to push their limits, overcome challenges, and achieve greatness. It emphasizes the brand's commitment to delivering high-performance athletic gear and motivating people to act and pursue their goals.

- **Coca-Cola, "Open Happiness":** Coca-Cola's big promise centers around the idea of spreading joy and happiness. The brand promises to deliver refreshing beverages that enhance moments of togetherness and create a positive emotional experience.

- **Airbnb, "Belong Anywhere":** Airbnb's big promise is to provide a platform where travelers can find unique accommodations and experience a sense of belonging wherever they go. It emphasizes the brand's commitment to creating a global community and fostering connections between hosts and guests.

- **Amazon, "Earth's Most Customer-Centric Company":** Amazon's big promise is to prioritize the needs and satisfaction of its customers above all else. The brand focuses on delivering convenience, selection, and a seamless shopping experience to enhance customer satisfaction and loyalty.

- **FedEx, "When It Absolutely, Positively Has to Be There Overnight":** FedEx's big promise revolves around the reliability and speed of its delivery services. The brand emphasizes its commitment to ensuring that time-sensitive shipments reach their destinations without fail, providing peace of mind to customers.

- **Google, "Organize the World's Information and Make It Universally Accessible and Useful":** Google's big promise centers around organizing and delivering information in a way that is accessible and valuable to users worldwide. The brand aims to provide the most relevant and comprehensive search results and services.

Of course, we aren't Apple, we aren't Nike. We don't have billions of dollars to invest in marketing over multiple years to make our big promise stick and make sense. So how do we make a big promise work for us? We have to make it specific. A big promise is the equivalent of a campaign slogan. When you decide to create a personal brand, you need a big promise for your brand. This is a statement to the world of the value you deliver. The more specific your big promise is, the more quickly you can land your message clearly with your Most Valuable Clients.

What Is a Personal Brand?

Imagine you're walking into a room filled with people. Each person has their own unique personality, style, and way of interacting with others. They leave an impression based on how they present themselves, how they communicate, and the value they bring to the conversation. That's essentially what a personal brand is – it's what you want people to remember about you.

Your personal brand is the essence of who you are, both personally and professionally. It's how you present yourself to the world, how you differentiate yourself from others, and how you showcase your unique qualities and expertise. Your personal brand is what sets you apart from the competition and establishes you as a credible and trustworthy authority in your field.

Now, you might be thinking, "But I'm not a celebrity or a public figure, so why do I need a personal brand?"

Here's the thing—personal branding is not just for celebrities or influencers. It's for anyone who wants to make a lasting impression and stand out in a crowded marketplace. Whether you're a solopreneur, a freelancer, or even an employee within a company, your personal brand matters.

Why does it matter? Well, think about it. When you're looking to hire a service or buy a product, who do you trust more—a faceless business or a person who has established themselves as an expert and has built a strong personal brand?

Most likely, it's the latter.

People connect with people. People buy from people, not from logos or generic company names.

Your personal brand helps you build trust, establish credibility, and develop meaningful relationships with your audience or customers. It allows you to showcase your expertise, share your unique story, and communicate your values and passions. The reason people will choose you is not just because of the outcome and process, but also who you are as an individual and a business.

It doesn't matter how great an expert you are; if people can't gel with you, they won't buy from you.

In a noisy and competitive world, having a strong personal brand helps you cut through the clutter and capture the attention of the right people. Using your personal brand online and in person is easier than ever now. You have social media, online events, podcasts, blogs, and all the offline opportunities. There is no doubt, however, that the fastest way to build a personal brand and be known as the go-to person is online. You can reach 10 times more people than you can offline.

How Do You Build a Personal Brand?

It starts with self-reflection. Take the time to define who you are, what you stand for, and what you want to be known for as an individual. Think about your values, your strengths, and the unique

51

qualities that make you special. Your personal brand is a combination of who you are as a person, your message to the market (big promise), and of course the services you offer. When you build your personal brand, you become your business's biggest marketing asset.

One interesting way to think about personal branding is looking to Hollywood. When a movie studio is working on a new project, they hire a casting director to find the right people for the parts in the film. If you look at most of the blockbuster films, they've hired actors who were known for a particular genre and have had blockbuster roles before. Some of our famous Hollywood names have made a living playing very similar roles in films for decades. The actor almost makes a film a "safe bet" for an audience.

There are many actors in a genre, but they all have their unique style and flair. Even actors who play action-hero roles differ massively. When casting directors are researching potential actors for lead roles, they compare many different people all in the same genre but have different styles. Their job is to work out who fits with the vision the studio has for the film.

Our personal brand is no different. We might be in a crowded market, but we have to bring our unique way of doing things, our style, to our personal brand to differentiate ourselves from others. This is what personal branding is. It's about defining yourself for a specific role, and injecting into that role your worldview, style, and expertise, so the audience knows what to expect.

Your personal brand will attract people who like your way. Your personal brand builds off of your big promise. If your big promise is the outcome you deliver, your personal brand is the way in which you do it.

Understanding your personal brand is absolutely key to portraying your unique value and identity. Here are some questions that can help you define your own personal brand:

- **What are my core values?** These are the guiding principles that dictate your behavior and action.

- **What are my strengths and unique skills?** These are your key abilities that set you apart from others.

- **What are my passions?** What do you love to do? Your passions often align with your purpose.

- **What are my goals?** Both short-term and long-term goals give direction to your personal brand.

- **How do others perceive me?** This gives an external perspective on your brand.

- **What are your pet hates within your industry or niche?** These will help you define yourself based on how you view the solutions to clients' problems.

- **What words would you use to describe your personality and communication style?** These help you inject your personality into your marketing and avoid you being generic.

- **How do I want to be perceived?** This is your desired brand image.

- **What are my personal experiences and how have they shaped me?** Personal experiences often influence your unique perspective and values.

- **What are my weaknesses or areas for improvement?** Recognizing these helps refine your brand and ensure you work on weaknesses and play to your strengths.

- **What are the key achievements in my life?** Achievements often highlight your skills and ambitions.

- **What type of culture or environment do I thrive in?** This can reveal a lot about your preferred work style and personality.

Repetition Is Powerful, Even When You Think It's Annoying

Repetition is a fundamental element of effective personal branding and marketing. By consistently presenting the same message across multiple channels and over time, you can reinforce your brand identity and become known for a specific expertise or offering. In fact, repetition is crucial for brand recognition and recall, which can significantly impact a consumer's decision-making process. However, it is essential to strike a balance between reinforcing your message and oversaturating your audience.

As you build your personal brand, it is natural to worry about sounding repetitive or redundant. You may feel that you are pushing the same message too often and that your audience may become bored or annoyed. However, the reality is that your audience is exposed to a vast amount of information every day, making it challenging for them to remember and associate your message with your brand.

In this context, the concept of the "mere exposure effect" comes into play. It is a psychological phenomenon in which people tend to develop a preference for things they are repeatedly exposed to. By consistently presenting your message, you can leverage this effect to build brand recognition and trust. Here are some reasons why repetition is so crucial in personal branding and marketing:

- **Capture Attention Amid Noise:** In today's digital age, people are inundated with information from multiple sources—social media, email, websites, advertisements, and more. Amid this noise, it is challenging for your message to stand out and be remembered. Repetition ensures that your audience encounters your message multiple times, increasing the likelihood of capturing their attention and imprinting your message in their memory.

- **Overcome the "Forgetting Curve":** The forgetting curve is a theory proposed by psychologist Hermann Ebbinghaus that describes how information is lost over time when it is not intentionally retained. Repetition helps combat this natural tendency to forget by continually reinforcing your message, making it more likely that your audience will remember your brand and what it stands for.

- **Build Trust Through Familiarity:** Familiarity breeds trust. The more your audience sees your message, the more familiar they become with your personal brand. This familiarity can lead to increased trust and credibility, as people tend to prefer and trust what they know over what is unfamiliar.

- **Increase Brand Consistency:** Repetition fosters consistency in your personal branding efforts. By delivering a consistent message across various platforms and over time, you reinforce your brand identity and ensure that your audience receives a coherent and unified perception of your brand.

- **Drive Action:** Repetition can help drive your audience to take action. The more often your audience encounters your message, the more likely they are to take the desired action, whether it be subscribing to your newsletter, purchasing your product, or attending your event.

It is essential to understand that you may tire of your message long before your audience does. As the creator of your personal brand, you are likely far more familiar with your messaging than your audience is. This discrepancy can lead to the false belief that your audience has heard your message enough, when in reality they may just be starting to take notice. It is crucial to remember that your audience's exposure to your message is likely far less frequent than your own.

However, you need to balance repetition with variety, ensuring that your message remains engaging and relevant. The key is to persist in sharing your message even when you feel like you have repeated it enough, because that may be the moment when your audience is just starting to take notice.

Can I Create a Personal Brand?

Let me guess: you don't feel famous enough or confident enough to build a personal brand. Perhaps you feel like someone might think you are arrogant or self-centered. These are all common fears and concerns people have about building their own personal brand.

If you are worrying about these things, believe it or not, that's a good thing. It shows you want to build your personal brand authentically. Your concerns are valid and a good check and balance against pushing the envelope of personal branding too far.

But right now you are imagining the worst possible scenario, and that scenario is probably preventing you from taking any action. We can quickly obsess about minor things and make them a big deal.

We've all seen those people who self-promote and overcook it. Nobody wants to do that, but over time, if you see that a lot, you can slip into believing the myth that personal branding is overexaggerated and full of fake personas. So let's dispel those myths now.

Busting Common Myths About Personal Branding

Personal branding is the process of creating and maintaining a unique and consistent image or identity for an individual, typically to enhance their professional reputation and build their credibility. It involves marketing yourself and your career as a brand. In the age of social media and the gig economy, personal branding has become increasingly important for professionals and entrepreneurs alike.

However, there are several myths and misconceptions surrounding personal branding that can be misleading and counterproductive. Here, we debunk some of the most common myths.

Myth 1: Personal Branding Is Only for Celebrities or High-Profile Individuals

One of the most pervasive myths is that personal branding is only for celebrities, influencers, or high-profile individuals. While it's true that well-known figures often have carefully cultivated personal brands, personal branding is essential for everyone, regardless of their fame or profession. In today's digital age, employers, clients, and colleagues will likely search for you online, making it crucial for individuals at all career stages to have a strong and consistent personal brand. A positive personal brand can enhance your reputation, establish your expertise, and open up new opportunities.

Myth 2: Personal Branding Is Just About Self-Promotion

Another common myth is that personal branding is all about shameless self-promotion. While promoting yourself is part of personal branding, it is far from the whole story. Personal branding is about authenticity, consistency, and value. It involves creating and sharing valuable content, engaging with your audience, and building genuine relationships. Your personal brand should reflect who you are, what you stand for, and how you can help others. It's about creating a positive and lasting impression that resonates with your target audience.

Myth 3: Personal Branding Requires You to Be an Expert in Everything

Some people believe that to have a strong personal brand, they need to be experts in every aspect of their field. This is simply not true.

In fact, trying to be an expert in everything can be counterproductive. Personal branding is about showcasing your unique strengths, skills, and experiences. Focus on your niche or areas where you have expertise, and share your insights and knowledge with your audience. By being authentic and providing valuable content, you can establish yourself as a trusted authority in your field.

Myth 4: Personal Branding Is All About Your Online Presence

While your online presence plays a significant role in personal branding, it is not the only factor. Personal branding encompasses your entire professional identity, including your offline interactions, behavior, and communication. Your personal brand should be consistent across all platforms and touchpoints. Remember that every interaction you have, both online and offline, contributes to your personal brand. Ensure that your actions align with the image you want to project.

Myth 5: Personal Branding Means You Can't Show Vulnerability

Some people think that personal branding requires them to project an image of perfection. In reality, showing vulnerability and authenticity can make you more relatable and human. Sharing your challenges, struggles, and mistakes can help you connect with your audience on a deeper level. It's essential to strike a balance between showcasing your successes and being open about your vulnerabilities. Authenticity is a key element of personal branding.

Myth 6: Personal Branding Is Set in Stone

A common misconception is that once you establish your personal brand, it cannot change or evolve. In reality, personal branding is an ongoing process, and your brand should evolve as you grow personally and professionally. As your skills, experiences, and interests change, your personal brand should reflect these developments. Don't be afraid to update your personal brand to align with your current values, goals, and expertise.

Myth 7: Personal Branding Is a Time-Consuming Process

Many people believe that personal branding requires a significant time investment. While building a strong personal brand does require effort, it doesn't have to be time-consuming. By integrating personal branding into your daily routine, you can make incremental progress without overwhelming yourself. Sharing your insights, engaging with your audience, and updating your online profiles are all steps you can take in just a few minutes each day.

Myth 8: Personal Branding Is Only for Individuals in Certain Professions

Some people think that personal branding is only relevant for individuals in certain professions, such as marketing, sales, or entrepreneurship. In reality, personal branding is important for professionals in all fields and industries. Whether you're an engineer, teacher, artist, or healthcare professional, personal branding can help you stand out, build credibility, and advance your career.

Myth 9: Personal Branding Is Only About Making Money

While personal branding can certainly help you attract clients, customers, or job offers, it's not just about making money. Personal branding is about building a reputation, establishing your expertise, and creating meaningful connections. By focusing on providing value, sharing your knowledge, and building relationships, you can create a personal brand that benefits both you and your audience.

Myth 10: Personal Branding Is a Solo Effort

Some people think that personal branding is a solo effort, but it's essential to involve others in the process. Seek feedback from trusted colleagues, mentors, or friends. Engage with your audience, respond to their comments, and collaborate with others in your industry. Building relationships and networking are critical components of personal branding.

Authenticity Matters

It's important to stress that your personal brand is about accurately defining your uniqueness and expertise for your target audience. It's about you being authentic and conveying clearly. Too often, people create personal brands online that are fake or don't come from a place of authenticity. They think they need to be someone else in order to be successful. The key to a successful personal brand is to be your true self.

Of course, we are complex creatures, so a personal brand will never fully convey the depth of our personality. But it will help us more clearly help our audience see our uniqueness and draw people who resonate with our personal brands.

Chapter 5

Getting Organized and Systemizing Your Growth

You won't grow unless you've got a system. For sustained business growth, it is essential to have a written plan of action outlining how you will generate inquiries and win new clients. Without it, you will find yourself bouncing around, struggling to get anything to work.

Having worked in this field for a long time, I can offer you the most important piece of advice I've ever received: Nothing works out of the box. As you develop a process to go from complete strangers to paying clients, you'll need to refine it over time. It's perfectly normal. Although many people believe things should be easier, they only get easier as you become more proficient.

Over the years, I've had the pleasure of speaking with thousands of business owners. In doing so, I've identified several common issues and challenges that arise when building a system for business growth. I want to share them with you, so you can avoid the pain, wasted time, and wasted money that come with these pitfalls.

Searching for the Missing Puzzle Piece

We live in a time when opportunities are abundant, and the world is at our fingertips. However, this has also fostered a culture of instant gratification. On social media and the internet, we are constantly exposed to stories of people becoming millionaires in a matter of days.

While these success stories are inspiring, they can also make us feel as though something is missing in our own lives.

As a result, we search for the elusive "missing piece of the puzzle," the secret trick or hack that will catapult our business to new heights. I've met individuals who have spent years, even decades, and thousands of dollars in pursuit of that shortcut. Ironically, they end up spending years trying to find a way to save time.

The truth is that building a successful business requires a systematic approach. It's about developing a system, refining it, and working it tirelessly. Most growing businesses experience a "flywheel effect," where their actions fuel growth. Their marketing efforts increase awareness, leading to opportunities that feed into a cycle of sales and marketing. In this cycle, sales generate revenue, which is then reinvested into marketing, creating a self-sustaining loop that propels the business forward.

The allure of instant gratification poses a significant challenge for many business owners. In their quest for quick wins and easy answers, they become fixated on finding the missing piece of the puzzle. I once met a successful lawyer who ran his own practice, employing many people and making good money. However, he was always searching for something more, something that would provide him with a massive payday.

Although he had all the trappings of a comfortable life, he continued to seek business opportunities internationally and partnerships with others. His law practice was funding these speculative ventures, but he wasn't investing any energy or resources into growing his core business. Unfortunately, this lack of attention eventually led to the closure of his firm.

Now, you might be thinking, "I would never do that." But I see business owners falling into this trap all the time. They dabble in various marketing strategies, from social media to blogging to email marketing, without ever fully committing to any one approach.

This lack of focus results in nothing really working for them because they haven't invested enough time and effort into perfecting a single system.

The reality is that slow progress doesn't necessarily indicate a problem. Marketing is a long-term investment that often yields compound benefits. As a solopreneur, it can be challenging to balance client work with consistent marketing efforts, but it's crucial to keep the momentum going. The marketing you do today will likely pay off in 90 days, so it's essential to stick with it.

Having a well-defined system for sales and marketing is essential for predictable revenue. If you find yourself in a cycle of good months followed by rough ones, it's a telltale sign that you lack a consistent sales and marketing system. So make the time for marketing, establish a plan, and build a system that will create a predictable flow of revenue for your business. Having a well-defined system is the real puzzle piece you've been looking for.

Diarizing Your Actions

One of the worst things you can do is get a list of tasks and not allocate time to do them. The growth of your business will always play second fiddle for as long as you don't give it a slot in your working week.

I learned early on that there will always be something to do that will give you a legitimate reason to "do marketing later." The problem is, as a business owner, you'll always have a to-do list bigger than your capacity. Business owners, by their nature, are inventive people, so you'll always have more on your plate than you can handle. It goes with the job. So you either need to set a regimented slot in your diary or allocate tasks time in your working week.

One of my challenges has always been time management. I'm really bad at time management and despite two decades of business experience, I'm still working on it. I know that if I try to do my marketing activity during the business day, I will get nothing done. I plan all my marketing activities between 6 a.m. and 8 a.m. each day. That probably sounds crazy to some, but it works for me. I can get the key marketing tasks done before my day starts and so I know when I finish my day, I have made time for the things that will make me money.

I could, of course, do it at the end of the day, but my energy levels fall off a cliff once we reach 2–3 p.m. By locking in that time each morning and assigning work to the slots, I protect the time.

In my slots in the morning, I'm creating content, writing emails, and developing ideas. I use the Eisenhower matrix to prioritize my time. I do this because I'm a sucker for doing the fun stuff and leaving the hard work for "later."

You know what I mean, because you do it too. I love designing things, so if I have a design task, I'll want to do that first. I'll burn through two hours on Canva, then leave myself no more marketing time for that day. This is human nature to try and do the easiest or most enjoyable thing first.

Trust me, you want to tackle the work that will make the most difference. What are the most important things that will make the biggest difference? Pick those off your list first.

The Eisenhower Matrix

Imagine you're standing in front of a messy room. Everywhere you look, there are piles of tasks demanding your attention. Some are urgent but not important, like a ringing phone. Others are crucial for your long-term success but not pressing, like planning your future. How do you decide where to start?

The Eisenhower Matrix, also known as the Urgent-Important Matrix, is a time management tool used to prioritize tasks based on their urgency and importance. Rooted in a principle attributed to

President Dwight D. Eisenhower, it distinguishes between tasks that require immediate attention and those vital for long-term success.

The matrix is divided into four quadrants:

1. **Urgent and Important:** This quadrant encompasses tasks that are both immediate and crucial. Typically, these are reactive tasks, like urgent work deadlines or emergencies. Addressing them is essential, and they should be attended to immediately.

2. **Not Urgent but Important:** Tasks in this quadrant are significant for long-term goals but lack the urgency of those in Quadrant I. They might include activities such as personal and professional development, long-term planning, or building relationships. The challenge is to schedule and prioritize these tasks effectively since they can be easily overshadowed by more urgent matters.

3. **Urgent but Not Important:** This quadrant contains tasks that appear to demand immediate attention but don't significantly contribute to our major goals. These tasks often arise due to other people's priorities. Whenever possible, consider delegating these tasks or addressing them in a time-efficient manner.

4. **Not Urgent and Not Important:** Activities here offer little in terms of achieving meaningful goals. They can be distractions or habits, like mindless internet browsing. It's advised to reduce or eliminate tasks from this quadrant to focus on more meaningful activities.

I decided to make my own version of the Eisenhower Matrix so I could prioritize the tasks and activities that will help me grow and build my business. (See Figure 5.1.) Without setting your priorities and documenting them you rely on your memory, and it's easy to

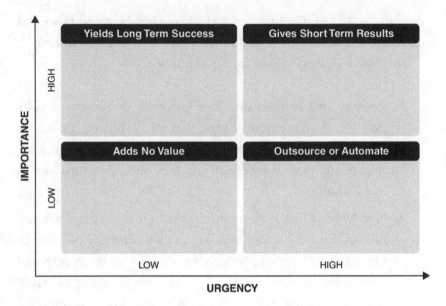

Figure 5.1 A Variation on the Eisenhower Matrix

forget important things that aren't urgent, then suddenly realize that your long-term priorities are neglected.

Focusing on Long-Term Success

When you're aiming for lasting success in your business, focusing on strategies that yield long-term benefits is crucial. These activities generally bear fruit over time and don't have "quick wins."

Here's an insight into activities that can anchor your growth:

- **Content Marketing:** Investing in content that resonates with your target audience helps in building trust and positioning yourself as a leader in the industry.

- **Personal Branding:** Crafting a consistent and authentic personal brand sets you apart from the competition. It tells your unique story and builds a connection with the audience.

- **Building a Social Media Presence:** A strong social media presence allows you to engage with your audience, understand their needs, and provide timely responses, fostering long-term relationships.

- **Google Reviews and Trustpilot Rankings:** Positive reviews on platforms like Google and Trustpilot enhance your online reputation. Encourage satisfied customers to leave reviews, and respond to feedback to build trust and transparency.

- **Growing Your Email List:** An email list is a valuable asset for personalized communication. Focus on growing this list through valuable content and exclusive offers to maintain ongoing engagement with your customers.

- **Website SEO:** Optimizing your website for search engines ensures that potential customers can find you when they're looking for products or services in your niche. Regular updates with quality content and strategic keyword placement are vital for maintaining visibility.

- **Referral Programs:** Encouraging referrals from satisfied customers creates a self-sustaining cycle of growth, enhancing both immediate and long-term sales.

- **Continuous Learning and Adaptation:** Regularly assess and adjust your strategies to ensure relevance in an ever-evolving business landscape.

- **Value Proposition:** Offering lasting value rather than quick fixes ensures that customers come back and advocate for your brand.

- **Training and Development:** A well-trained sales team equipped to understand customer needs deeply fosters long-term customer relationships.

A number of years ago, two very clever men—Les Binet and Peter Field—wrote a detailed analysis of what works in sales and marketing called *The Long and Short of It* (discussed below). I use some of their findings from their research in my own presentations.

Essentially, their book explains that many of the tactical things we can do to win new business often have very little long-term benefit. Likewise many of the brand-related things we can do, like building our personal brand or developing our online presence, have a more profitable long-term benefit.

Binet and Fielding's book summarizes that you need a blend of both activities to really achieve long-term growth. It's almost impossible to scale a business with tactical marketing and sales. That's why many businesses struggle to grow: The balance between long-term and short-term benefits are out of balance. Too much short term, and you don't create the awareness and trust you need to attract inbound interest. Too little short term, and you'll go out of business.

It's all about balance.

Avoiding Short-Term Results

Short-term results are things that can affect your revenue in the next 90 days. These are things you should be doing daily and weekly to achieve your short-term revenue goals.

Before we get into the list, let's just discuss the risk of not focusing on the long term and sticking with short-term goals.

First, if you focus on short-term goals, you'll get fewer inbound leads and opportunities. Inbound leads are the gold elixir of marketing. Inbound leads convert more effectively and will help you spend less time selling.

Second, relying too much on short-term activity will never allow you to build your long-term business; you'll always be operating in the short term. That means your revenue will be more unpredictable and it will be challenging for you to invest in your continued growth.

Where would you rather be: one step ahead, or ten?

Here are many of the tasks that produce short-term results:

- **Flash Sales and Discounts:** Limited-time offers create a sense of urgency and can drive immediate sales.

- **Pay-Per-Click Advertising:** Targeted advertising campaigns can quickly draw attention to specific products or services.

- **Social Media Ad Campaigns:** Platforms like Facebook and Instagram allow for highly targeted advertising that can yield quick results.

- **Cold Calling and Cold Outreach:** Reaching out to potential customers directly, even if they have not shown previous interest, can lead to quick sales.

- **Following Up on Existing Inquiries:** Responding promptly to enquiries from potential customers can convert interest into sales.

- **Contacting Old Customers:** Reconnecting with previous customers with special offers or updates on products they might like can reignite interest.

- **Upselling Existing Customers:** Offering complementary products or premium versions to current customers can enhance immediate revenue.

- **Influencer Partnerships:** Collaborating with influencers for product promotions can create instant visibility and engagement.

- **Email Marketing Campaigns:** Sending promotional emails to your existing subscribers about a new product, service, or offer can generate immediate interest.

- **Trade Shows and Exhibitions:** Participating in industry-specific events can put your products directly in front of a targeted audience.

- **Limited-Time Collaborations:** Collaborating with other brands for a limited period can generate buzz and interest.

- **Launching a New Product or Service:** The initial excitement around a new offering can lead to quick sales if adequately promoted.

- **Customer Testimonials:** Sharing positive feedback from satisfied customers can build immediate trust.

- **Retargeting Ads:** Targeting users who have previously interacted with your site but didn't make a purchase can lead to quick conversions.

- **Pop-up Shops or Stands:** Temporary physical locations can generate interest and immediate sales in a local area.

- **Contests and Giveaways:** These can rapidly increase brand visibility and engagement on platforms like social media.

- **Seasonal Promotions:** Offering special promotions during holidays or seasonal events can boost sales during those specific periods.

- **Networking:** Attending networking events in your local area can be a quick way to build relationships and create opportunities for your business.

A number of years ago, we hit a rough patch in our business. I needed to drum up a lot of new business quickly. I was in the middle of rebranding my business but a few things hadn't gone to plan.

As a result, I needed to rebuild the pipeline from scratch. I had to hit every short-term tactic I could over a three-month period. I was sending cold outreach, networking, and running promotions. I was working flat out to turn things around. This is what happens if you focus only on short-term opportunities.

Short-term tactics are brilliant if you need to take action quickly; they can fill a hole or provide a short-term lift in sales. That's why they are tactical. They aren't designed to win the war, but they could help you plug a short-term gap or help you get things moving.

When you start out in business, you have to do a lot of tactical activities to get momentum behind your business. As you grow and your business matures, you have to think more long-term, more strategic.

The two well-respected marketing leaders mentioned above, Les Binet and Peter Field, undertook a large-scale study published as *The Long and the Short of It: Balancing Short and Long-Term Marketing Strategies*. For people like me, it is gold dust. It helps explain what is working and where the sweet spot is between more strategic marketing and short-term marketing activities.

There are two elements of this report that really matter for us. The first is that long-term marketing benefits and short-term benefits are generated in very different ways. In that report the data from the IPA (Institute of Professional Advertisers) suggests that the optimum balance of long-term and short-term marketing activities should be 60:40.

So what does this mean for us? Put simply, we need a mix of activity. Short term can help us right now, but it's hard to grow consistently using short-term tactics; likewise, trying to build a brand is a longer-term strategy, which will have long-term payoff, but in the short term might feel like a lot of effort for little reward.

Eliminating Activities That Add No Value

In the ever-competitive world of sales and marketing, every activity you undertake should serve a clear purpose. Are you conducting certain marketing practices simply because "it's the way things have always been done"? Are there sales tactics that you feel obliged to follow but you can't point to any discernible benefits? If these questions strike a chord, it's time for a comprehensive review of your marketing and sales activities.

It's not uncommon to find practices that have become deeply entrenched in a company's routine but no longer align with either short-term or long-term objectives. These activities can suck your valuable time, energy, and resources without contributing to your bottom line. In the dynamic landscape of today's business world, such practices can hinder rather than help. Therefore, a ruthless evaluation of these activities is not just wise, but essential.

Step 1: Identify the Activities. The first step is to identify all the marketing and sales activities your business engages in. Make a comprehensive list and include everything, even those tasks that seem insignificant.

Step 2: Evaluate Short- and Long-Term Impact. Once you've identified all the activities, assess each one for its short- and long-term impact. If you find that an activity is not contributing to immediate sales or building your brand over time, it's a clear indicator that it might need to be eliminated.

Step 3: Consider the "Why." Ask yourself, why are these activities still part of the routine? Is it tradition, peer pressure, or perhaps an inherited practice from predecessors? Understanding the underlying reason can be enlightening and make the decision to cut the activity more justified.

Step 4: Analyze the Costs. Consider the financial, time, and human resource costs associated with these noncontributing activities. You might be surprised at how much you're investing in practices that provide no return on investment.

Step 5: Be Ruthless but Thoughtful. Eliminating a long-standing practice can be challenging, and there might be resistance from your team. Approach this with clear communication about why the change is happening and what the expected benefits are. Being thoughtful but firm in your decision-making process will ensure a smoother transition.

Step 6: Redirect Resources. With the newfound time and resources, you now have the opportunity to invest in activities that align with your business goals. Whether focusing on targeted advertising, relationship building, or expanding into new markets, the redirection can reinvigorate your marketing and sales strategies.

Step 7: Monitor and Adjust. Finally, this process shouldn't be a one-time effort. Regularly review your marketing and sales activities to ensure that they are continually aligned with your business objectives. This ongoing vigilance will keep your strategies fresh and effective.

You're not alone if you find this concept intimidating. It's a bold step to cut what might have been a foundational part of your business routine. However, the benefits are undeniable.

By eliminating time-consuming and ineffective practices, you free up resources to invest in strategies that will get you to your goals. It's a courageous move that demands honest self-reflection and a commitment to innovation and growth.

Outsource or Automate

Your time is precious. What if you had a little more of that precious resource every day? Imagine if you could direct your focus towards what you're truly good at, allowing others to handle tasks that drain your time. This is where outsourcing and automation come into play.

Outsourcing: Leverage Expertise and Get More Done

The beauty of the internet era is that you don't have to do everything yourself. Platforms like Upwork and Fiverr have changed the game, giving you access to talented professionals who can handle various aspects of your business, freeing up your time and energy.

- **Graphic Design:** Need a stunning logo or engaging social media visuals? Instead of struggling with design software, hire an expert to craft the visual aesthetics that resonate with your brand.

- **Website Building:** You're good at selling, but web development might not be your cup of tea. Hire a website builder to create a sleek, user-friendly site that reflects your business persona.

- **Creating Social Media Content:** Content is king, but creation is time-consuming. Engage a social media expert to curate and create posts that speak your brand's language.

- **Editing Videos:** Video content is vital in today's market. Outsourcing video editing ensures your visuals are crisp and professional, without spending endless hours in editing software.

- **Copywriting:** Your message needs to be clear, compelling, and in line with your brand's voice. A skilled copywriter can articulate your ideas in a way that resonates with your audience.

Automating: Do More with Less

Now let's talk about automating those repetitive tasks that eat into your valuable time. Automation tools are not just time-savers; they're strategic partners in efficiency.

- **Calendly:** You're constantly juggling meetings and appointments, right? Calendly can automate booking into your diary, eliminating the endless back-and-forth emails.

- **Zapier:** This tool can help you connect different software together, creating seamless workflows that save both time and money. Imagine all your favorite tools talking to each other, working in harmony!

- **Setting Reminders for Calls with Prospects:** Automated reminders ensure you never miss a call. It's like having a virtual assistant keeping track of your schedule.

- **Using a CRM to Track Prospects:** CRMs are not just databases; they're relationship builders. Automated follow-up prompts mean you never lose sight of a potential client.

You're now looking at a world where you can have more control over your time and where your skills are most needed. Understanding the value of your time means recognizing that some tasks are better left to others or to automated systems.

Why spend hours on tasks that others can perform more efficiently? Focus on what you do best: the higher-value work that drives your business forward. Outsourcing and automation are not just about saving time; they're about smart business management.

Chapter 6

Reducing Sales Friction

I know firsthand how challenging selling can be. It doesn't matter if you've been in the game for years or if you're just starting out—selling is tough. Selling cold is the toughest gig I've ever done. Trying to move people from "I don't know you" to "I'm interested in buying from you" in a very short period requires a lot of skill and a very thick skin.

As a small business owner or solopreneur, you already have a million other tasks on your plate. Trying to convince clients to buy your products or services can feel soul-destroying, time-consuming, and even downright terrifying at times. You don't want to be trying to sell cold. You want as little friction in the sales process as possible. That's where marketing comes in. Marketing is the secret sauce that can make your services appealing, attractive, and easier to sell.

Reducing friction in selling can be broken down into three key parts: awareness, relatability, and belief.

First, awareness is all about ensuring that your prospects are familiar with your business. You need to capture their attention and make them aware of what you have to offer. After all, if they don't know you exist, they can't buy from you. Effective marketing strategies can help raise awareness and get your business on the radar of potential clients.

Next, we have relatability. Your prospects need to be able to relate to you and your brand. They should feel a connection, an understanding that you truly recognize their pain points and can provide solutions. Building relatability through your marketing efforts helps establish a strong bond and creates a sense of trust between you and your potential clients.

Finally, belief plays a crucial role in the selling process. Your prospects need to believe in your business and the value you provide. Building trust is paramount in gaining their confidence and overcoming any skepticism or doubts they may have. Your marketing should focus on showcasing your expertise, credibility, and delivering on your promises.

Think of these three components as part of your election campaign. Your voters are your potential clients. Just like political candidates vying for votes, as a business owner or solopreneur, you are competing for the attention and loyalty of your target audience. Understanding the parallels between marketing and election campaigns can provide valuable insights into how to effectively reach and engage your potential customers.

Both marketing and election campaigns are centered around a big promise or vision—your outcome. In politics, candidates rally around a specific agenda or set of values that they believe will benefit the constituents. Similarly, in marketing, you need to clearly articulate the big promise or outcome that your products or services can deliver to your target audience. This promise is what sets you apart from your competitors and serves as the driving force behind your marketing efforts.

Just like political campaigns, successful marketing requires raising awareness and visibility. In elections, candidates need to ensure that their message reaches as many voters as possible. They invest in advertising, public appearances, and media coverage to increase their visibility and make their agenda known. Similarly, in marketing, you must find ways to raise awareness of your brand, products, and services. This can be achieved through various channels such as social media, content marketing, advertising, and participating in industry events. The more you can increase your visibility and make your presence known to your target audience, the greater your chances of attracting their attention and interest.

Another similarity between marketing and election campaigns is the importance of relatability. Politicians understand the need to connect with voters on a personal level, to understand their concerns, and present themselves as relatable figures. Similarly, in marketing, you must establish a connection with your target audience. You need to understand their pain points, desires, and aspirations. By crafting your messaging and content in a way that resonates with your audience, you can establish a sense of relatability and build trust. This connection becomes the foundation for establishing long-lasting relationships with your customers.

Election candidates must build trust in their promises, marketers must build trust in their products or services. In an election, candidates must convince voters that they will follow through on their campaign promises and deliver the changes they envision. In marketing, you must provide evidence, testimonials, case studies, and social proof to demonstrate that you can deliver on your big promise. Building trust is crucial for overcoming skepticism and hesitation that potential customers may have.

Additionally, both marketing and election campaigns require effective communication and messaging. Politicians carefully craft their speeches, debates, and campaign materials to convey their vision and resonate with voters. Similarly, in marketing, you need to develop a clear and compelling message that communicates the value of your products or services. This message should be tailored to your target audience, addressing their specific needs and desires. By delivering a consistent and impactful message, you can capture the attention and interest of your potential customers.

So, as you embark on your marketing journey, think of yourself as a candidate running for office. You've got to build awareness, relatability, and belief.

Remember, you have only a limited amount of time and energy to invest. So concentrate your marketing efforts on your Most Valuable Clients and a clear desired outcome, and you can effectively eliminate friction from your sales process. By homing in on your market, you can position yourself as the go-to expert and communicate your value with clarity and confidence.

Awareness

You know, there's a saying that familiarity breeds contempt, but when it comes to marketing, that couldn't be further from the truth. In fact, the more aware your target audience is of who you are, the value you offer, and the services you provide, the easier your sales process becomes.

Big companies invest billions in awareness campaigns, and there's a good reason for that. Being known and top-of-mind with your target market is the key to driving long-term growth and success. Think about it—if your prospects are already familiar with your brand and what you bring to the table, you have less work to do when it comes to convincing them of your value.

Coca-Cola spends millions every year to make sure their drinks are top of mind. Awareness is everything. Building awareness is all about repetition. It's about finding creative ways to say the same things and ensuring that you're consistently visible to your prospects. I know it can be tempting to neglect this part of your marketing when you're swamped with work, but trust me, it's a mistake you don't want to make.

Let me share a personal example with you. I make it a point to post on social media every single day. Some days my posts perform exceptionally well, while other days they may not get as much traction. But here's the thing—I built my business on social media by consistently showing up and connecting with my ideal clients. Even if it feels like my efforts are going unnoticed at times, I know that being consistently seen is crucial for people to remember me as the go-to person in my industry.

I often talk about the concept of "lurkers" on social media—those individuals who see your content but don't necessarily engage with it. You'd be surprised by how many people silently follow your posts, getting immense value and getting to know you through your social media content alone. It's the kind of long-term awareness that pays off in unexpected ways.

I've had countless experiences where I've been invited to speak at events, and as I wrap up my talk and step off the stage, people approach me and share how they've been seeing my content in their feeds. They thank me for the tips and tricks I've shared, telling me how helpful they found them. It just goes to show that you never truly know who is seeing your marketing efforts and how it's impacting them.

The important thing to remember is that awareness cannot be neglected. It may not always deliver immediate results, but there's a time lag between the action you take and the effects it produces. Every effort you put into building awareness—whether it's adding value through social media content, attending events, networking, or engaging with industry groups—plays a significant role in establishing your presence and creating lasting impressions.

Now let's talk about some practical strategies you can implement to enhance your awareness-building efforts:

- Grow your following across your social media channels. Focus on increasing your reach and engaging with your target audience consistently.

- Post regularly and consistently across your social media channels. This ensures that you stay visible and maintain a consistent presence in the minds of your prospects.

- Engage with groups on social media that have your prospective clients as members. Join conversations, provide valuable insights, and establish yourself as a thought leader within those communities.

- Attend trade shows and conferences that are attended by your prospective clients. These events offer excellent networking opportunities and allow you to connect directly with your target audience.

- Consider hosting a podcast centered around key topics related to your service offering. This not only helps you reach a broader audience but also positions you as an authority in your field.

- Write informative and helpful blogs on your website, providing practical advice on key topics relevant to your audience. This demonstrates your expertise and builds trust with potential clients.

- Join relevant associations and trade bodies in your industry. This helps you gain credibility and opens doors to networking opportunities within your niche.

- Engage with and follow influencers in your prospective clients' industry. Collaborating with influencers or simply showing support for their work can expand your reach and attract the attention of their followers.

- Craft a speaker bio and offer to do free talks at industry-centric events. This allows you to share your expertise, connect with potential clients, and increase your visibility within your target market.

Relatability

Relatability is a powerful tool in business. It's all about creating a connection between you, as the business owner, and your potential customers. In a small business, this connection can be even more impactful because people are often more inclined to buy into the person behind the brand rather than the brand itself. Your personality, style, and the way you do business become significant factors that can influence someone's decision to purchase from you.

When it comes to relatability, authenticity is key. People want to see the real you, not just a polished image or a generic brand persona. They want to know who you are, what you stand for, and why you do what you do. By sharing your story, your values, and your journey as a business owner, you allow potential customers to see the human side behind the business. This transparency builds trust and makes it easier for people to relate to you on a personal level.

One of the common mistakes small business owners make is hiding behind their logo or trying to present a corporate façade. While branding is important, it should never overshadow the human element of your business. You are the biggest asset of your brand. By letting your personality shine through, you create a sense of familiarity and approachability that resonates with your audience.

Think about it: have you ever been drawn to a business because of the person running it? Have you felt a connection with someone based on their values or their approach to business? That's the power of relatability. When people like you and feel a connection with you, they are more likely to buy from you and support your business.

If you want to capitalize on social media to build your business, it is much easier to build your business around your personal profiles and accounts rather than a business profile. People buy from people, so it makes sense to leverage yourself to build your business.

It's about personality. In my own business, I have used my personal social media accounts to grow my business. It's worked well for us, and I get a steady stream of leads each day from my accounts. People can relate to another human more than a faceless business—so leverage your own identity to help your business.

Relatability is also about being relevant. You want people to see how your business and what you offer can make a difference in their lives. By understanding your target audience and their pain points, you can tailor your messaging and communication to address their specific needs. Show them that you understand their challenges and that your solutions are uniquely suited to help them overcome those challenges.

Building relatability takes time and effort, but the payoff is significant. It creates a loyal customer base and helps you stand out in a crowded market. It makes you unique. People want to do business with someone they can relate to, someone they trust and feel comfortable with. By infusing your marketing and communication with your unique personality, you create an authentic connection that goes beyond a transactional relationship.

Share your story, your values, and your passion. Be genuine and approachable. Show people why you are different and how your business can make a positive impact on their lives. Remember, in the world of small business, relatability is not just about your products or services; it's about you and the value you bring to the table.

Relatability refers to the ability to establish a connection or sense of commonality with others. It is the quality of being relatable or able to relate to the experiences, feelings, or situations of others. In the context of business and marketing, relatability is about creating a sense of familiarity and connection between your brand and your target audience.

When your business is relatable, it means that your audience can identify with your brand, values, and offerings. They see themselves in your story and feel that you understand their needs, challenges, and desires. Relatability is about showing empathy, understanding, and relevance to your target audience.

There are several ways to enhance relatability in your business:

- **Authenticity:** Be genuine and true to yourself and your brand. People appreciate honesty and transparency. Share your story, values, and personal experiences to connect on a deeper level with your audience.

- **Personalization:** Tailor your communication and marketing efforts to address the specific needs and preferences of your target audience. Show that you understand their unique challenges and provide solutions that resonate with them.

- **Storytelling:** Use storytelling techniques to convey your brand's message and values. Share narratives that evoke emotions and create a connection with your audience. Stories help humanize your brand and make it more relatable.

- **Use Real-Life Examples:** Incorporate real-life examples, case studies, or testimonials that demonstrate how your product or service has helped others. This allows your audience to see themselves in the success stories and envision the potential benefits for themselves.

- **Engage and Interact:** Foster two-way communication with your audience through social media, blog comments, or email newsletters. Encourage feedback, ask questions, and respond to comments. This creates a sense of community and shows that you value their input.

- **Show Your Personality:** Inject your personality into your brand communications. Let your unique voice and style shine through in your content, social media posts, and interactions.

This helps create an emotional connection and makes your brand more relatable.

- **Share Common Experiences:** Identify shared experiences or pain points that your audience can relate to. Address these common challenges and demonstrate how your product or service can provide a solution or improvement.

You can create a sense of connection, trust, and understanding with your target audience. When people feel that you understand them and their needs, they are more likely to engage with your brand, become loyal customers, and advocate for your business.

Belief

Belief is a strong conviction or acceptance that something is true, real, or reliable. In the context of business and marketing, belief refers to the confidence and trust that potential clients or customers have in your ability to deliver the promised outcomes or results.

When someone believes in your business, they have a deep-rooted faith that your product or service can solve their problems, meet their needs, or fulfill their desires. It goes beyond simply trusting that you will deliver what you promise; belief involves a strong conviction that your offering is effective, valuable, and capable of bringing about the desired outcomes.

Belief is often built through a combination of factors. Positive past experiences with your business, testimonials or case studies from satisfied clients, social proof in the form of reviews or endorsements, and consistent messaging that aligns with the values and goals of your target audience all contribute to establishing belief.

As a solopreneur, building belief in your offerings is crucial for attracting and retaining clients. When potential customers believe in what you offer, they are more likely to choose your product or service over alternatives, even if they come at a higher price. Belief can create a sense of confidence, reassurance, and certainty that their investment in your business will yield the desired outcomes.

It's important to note that belief is not just about making claims or promises; it requires delivering on those promises consistently and exceeding customer expectations. Building and maintaining belief requires providing high-quality products or services, excellent customer service, and ongoing support to ensure that the outcomes you promise are achieved.

Belief is a powerful driver of customer loyalty and advocacy. When your clients believe in your business, they become loyal customers who are more likely to refer your services to others, leave positive reviews, and become ambassadors for your brand. This positive word of mouth and reputation further strengthen belief in your business, attracting more potential customers.

Belief and trust are closely related concepts, but they have distinct differences. Trust is the reliance or confidence that someone has in the integrity, ability, or character of another person or entity. It involves a level of confidence and expectation that the other party will act in a reliable and trustworthy manner.

Belief, on the other hand, goes beyond trust. It is a deeper conviction or acceptance that something is true or real. It is a psychological state of accepting something as true or valid, often based on personal experiences, evidence, or a strong sense of conviction. Belief is about having faith in the capabilities, effectiveness, or value of a person, product, or idea.

In the context of business and marketing, trust is built on reliability, consistency, and the fulfillment of promises. It is earned through a track record of delivering on commitments, maintaining transparency, and acting in the best interest of the customer. Trust is crucial for establishing credibility and forming lasting relationships with clients.

Belief, on the other hand, is about the customer's perception of the potential outcomes or results that your business can provide. It goes beyond trusting that you will fulfill your promises; it involves a strong conviction that your offerings are effective, valuable, and capable of delivering the desired outcomes. Belief is often influenced by personal experiences, testimonials, social proof, and consistent messaging that aligns with the customer's goals and values.

While trust is important for establishing a foundation of reliability and credibility, belief takes it a step further by giving confidence and conviction in the customer's mind. Belief is an emotional and psychological state that creates a sense of certainty and assurance that your product or service will meet their needs or solve their problems.

- **Social Media Engagement:** Utilize social media platforms to engage with your target audience. Share valuable content, respond to comments and messages, and actively participate in relevant groups or communities. This helps create awareness and establishes you as an accessible and knowledgeable expert in your field.

- **Content Marketing:** Create and share valuable content through blog posts, videos, podcasts, or infographics. This positions you as an authority and builds relatability by addressing your audience's pain points and providing solutions. Consistently sharing valuable content helps establish trust and credibility over time.

- **Networking Events:** Attend industry-specific networking events, conferences, or trade shows to connect with potential clients or collaborators. Engage in meaningful conversations, share your expertise, and establish relationships. This face-to-face interaction builds awareness and creates relatability by allowing people to connect with you on a personal level.

- **Guest Blogging or Podcasting:** Seek opportunities to contribute guest articles to relevant blogs or be a guest on popular podcasts in your industry. This exposes you to new audiences, increases awareness of your brand, and positions you as an authority. It also helps build relatability by showcasing your expertise and providing valuable insights to a wider audience.

- **Testimonials and Case Studies:** Request testimonials from satisfied clients and showcase them on your website, social media, or marketing materials. Additionally, create case studies that demonstrate the positive outcomes your clients have achieved through your products or services. This social proof builds belief in your abilities and helps potential clients see the value you can deliver.

- **Personal Branding:** Develop a strong personal brand that aligns with your business. Share your story, values, and expertise authentically. Be consistent in your messaging and visuals across all platforms to create a recognizable and relatable brand image. Building a personal brand helps people connect with you and builds trust and belief in your offerings.

- **Thought Leadership:** Position yourself as a thought leader in your industry by sharing unique insights and perspectives. Publish articles on reputable industry websites, speak at conferences or events, and contribute to relevant publications. This establishes your expertise, builds credibility, and helps attract a wider audience who values your knowledge and insights.

- **Email Marketing:** Build an email list and regularly communicate with your subscribers. Provide valuable content, share updates, and offer exclusive promotions or discounts. This helps maintain awareness of your brand and keeps you top-of-mind with potential clients. Personalize your emails to create a sense of relatability and nurture belief in your offerings.

- **Collaborations and Partnerships:** Collaborate with other businesses or influencers in complementary industries. This allows you to tap into their existing audience and expand your reach. By aligning yourself with trusted and respected partners, you can enhance awareness, build relatability, and strengthen belief in your offerings.

Building awareness, relatability, and belief is an ongoing process. Consistency, authenticity, and delivering on your promises are key. By actively implementing these practical strategies, you can strengthen your business's presence, connect with your target audience, and cultivate belief in your offerings.

From Curious Prospects to Believing Fans

Curiosity is a powerful tool when it comes to attracting clients and driving sales. It has the ability to pique the interest of prospective clients and make them want to know more about what you have to offer. When curiosity is effectively employed in your sales and marketing efforts, it can lead potential clients to take those important first steps towards working with you.

Think about it—when you encounter something that piques your curiosity, you naturally feel drawn to explore it further. It's a natural human instinct to want to satisfy our curiosity and learn more about the things that capture our attention. This principle holds true in the world of business as well. By strategically incorporating curiosity into your marketing messages and materials, you can create an irresistible allure that compels prospective clients to want to know more about your products or services.

Curiosity plays a vital role in guiding potential clients through your sales and marketing funnel. By gradually unveiling information and offering enticing glimpses of what you have to offer, you can captivate their curiosity and draw them deeper into the process. This gradual approach allows potential clients to take baby steps, building trust and establishing a connection with your business over time.

Interestingly, when it comes to marketing, giving too much information can actually hinder your sales efforts. It may seem counterintuitive, but overwhelming potential clients with an abundance of details and information can lead to decision paralysis or confusion. There are limits to what you can effectively communicate in any marketing medium—be it a website, social media post, or email. By strategically using curiosity, you can create intrigue and leave your audience wanting more, compelling them to take the next step in the customer journey.

It's important to note that not all curiosity is created equal. While curiosity can attract interest and generate leads, it's crucial to foster focused curiosity rather than vague curiosity. Focused curiosity means attracting the attention of individuals who are genuinely interested in what you have to offer and align with your ideal client profile. This ensures that the leads and inquiries you receive are from individuals who are more likely to become valuable clients. On the other hand, vague curiosity can lead to time-wasting inquiries from individuals who are not the right fit for your business. It's essential to strike a balance and generate curiosity that is targeted and relevant to your specific niche.

By harnessing the power of curiosity in your marketing, you can create an engaging and compelling experience for potential clients. Craft your messages and materials in a way that ignites curiosity and leaves your audience eager to learn more. Offer teasers, snippets, and glimpses of the outcomes, solutions, or benefits that your products or services provide. As you guide them through the customer journey, gradually reveal more information and build on their curiosity to drive them towards making a purchasing decision.

Awareness, relatability, and belief unlock the power of curiosity to unlock leads and inquiries.

Education-Based Selling Certainty

One of the great tools you can have in your arsenal to help you grow your business is your knowledge. We often think of our knowledge and expertise as what helps us do our jobs, but it can also be a powerful marketing tool.

If you are helping customers, you're solving their problems. What is a difficult issue for them, you deal with every day. What seems like a new issue for them is commonplace to you. Don't take for granted the knowledge acquired. Don't assume it is common knowledge.

Over the years, I've used education-based selling to help me build trust and win business. All around the world right now, companies are hosting events and education-based events as a sales and marketing tool. When I launched my social selling business, I booked out physical venues in the UK and US to offer free training and support to small business owners. I gave a ton of value away because I knew it was key to building trust. I was hosting an event per week somewhere in the world and I do this to this day. It's proven very lucrative too. On average, I'm making a $6,000 profit from every location I visit.

When the pandemic came along, my events were shelved. So I did the same thing online. I hosted online live training webinars using LinkedIn and YouTube. Instead of getting 60 people per event, I'm now getting 600 per event.

Now, as you're reading this, you'll be concerned that you might give away some prize gem, which means people don't need to buy from you. It doesn't work that way. You see, customers don't buy our knowledge; they buy the outcome. Whenever a client signs up with me, they aren't buying more information; they are buying certainty about their transformation.

We fear we might say too much or inspire our prospects to do it without us, but in reality the opposite is true. By giving value and educating the prospect, we change the relationship from seller to teacher. This increases the certainty prospects have in our services, certainty it will help them achieve the outcome they desire.

When you wrap up reading this, you'll see everywhere you look a business using education-based selling and wonder why you've not been doing it.

Education-based selling is a powerful way to reduce the sales friction between you and your prospects. If you are known and trusted and your prospect has tasted the value of your knowledge and expertise, that makes your sales calls more relaxed and more likely to close.

Chapter 7

Social Selling: Leveraging Social Media Without Becoming an Influencer

Social selling is all about leveraging the power of social media to promote and generate business opportunities. It's a strategy that allows you to utilize platforms like Facebook, Instagram, LinkedIn, and others to engage with potential clients and convert those interactions into meaningful offline conversations and sales calls.

Social selling is one of the main topics I speak about in live events because it's so easy and yet so confusing. The rise of social media influencers and content creators has confused what social selling really is.

Many think it's about sending lots of sales messages online or documenting your life online; others think it's about attracting clients with content. In reality, social selling is neither of those, and both of those. Social selling is about building relationships online through content, personal branding, and sales outreach—it's a hybrid of all three. People buy from people they know, like, and trust. (See Figure 7.1.)

When we look back to around 2018, social selling was still relatively new in the sales and marketing world. It's only in recent years that social media has become a viable tool for winning business and reaching decision-makers who were previously inaccessible. The beauty of social media is that it enables us to connect with and reach a far greater number of people on a daily basis than we could ever

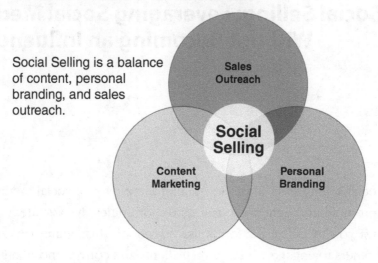

Social Selling is not the same as being a **Content Creator** or an **Influencer.**

Social Selling is a balance of content, personal branding, and sales outreach.

Sales Outreach

Social Selling

Content Marketing

Personal Branding

Figure 7.1 Clarifying Social Selling

do in person. The potential to connect with hundreds of individuals every day, without even leaving our office, is what makes social selling so compelling.

Essentially, social selling revolves around building relationships on social media platforms and leveraging those connections to create business opportunities. Let me share a personal experience to illustrate the power of social selling. Back in 2012, I was given the task of selling event tickets for a special community event at Wembley Stadium in the United Kingdom. The challenge was to sell 40,000 tickets in just seven weeks, with no budget for advertising. This meant that I had to rely solely on social selling to achieve this ambitious goal.

I turned to Facebook and began sending friend requests, engaging in conversations, and messaging individuals to inform them about the event. As part of the campaign, I introduced a concept called "bring a coach," where we approached organizations and asked if they would be interested in bringing a group of attendees. Through this organic social selling approach, we managed to sell an impressive 38,683 tickets without spending a dime on ads. This success story demonstrates the tremendous potential of social selling, as it allowed us to reach a vast audience that we otherwise would never have connected with. Moreover, it showcased the scalability and cost-effectiveness of this strategy, as we achieved remarkable results without any monetary investment.

Social selling costs you nothing but your time and commitment. Personally, I dedicate a significant portion of my day to social selling on my main platforms, which are Instagram and LinkedIn. These platforms have become powerhouses for social selling, particularly for small businesses. The beauty of it is that everyone is on these platforms, presenting a tremendous opportunity to connect, engage, and seize business opportunities.

To sum it up, social selling is a strategy that leverages social media platforms to promote and win business. It involves creating valuable content, expanding your network of followers, connections, or friends (depending on the platform), engaging in meaningful conversations, and ultimately converting those interactions into offline sales calls. The power of social selling lies in its ability to connect with individuals you may never meet in person, scale your reach, and spread your message widely—all at no financial cost. By dedicating your time and utilizing the potential of platforms like Instagram and LinkedIn, you can harness the immense power of social selling and unlock new avenues for business growth.

The Proper Focus of Social Selling

You don't need to be a social media influencer with thousands of followers to build your business through social selling. I completely agree with that sentiment. Many people think that social selling is only for those with massive followings and high influencer status, but the truth is that anyone, regardless of their follower count, can leverage social media to grow their business.

Let me explain why being a social media influencer isn't a prerequisite for success in social selling. While having a large following can certainly help in terms of reach and visibility, the real power of social selling lies in its ability to connect with the right audience and build meaningful relationships. It's not about the quantity of followers, but the quality of connections you make.

When it comes to social selling, the focus should be on engaging with your target audience, your most valuable clients, rather than trying to amass a huge following. It's about identifying the people who would benefit the most from your products or services and actively engaging with them through valuable content and personalized interactions.

In fact, having a smaller, highly engaged audience can be more beneficial than having a large following that lacks genuine interest in your offerings. By concentrating on building relationships and delivering value to a smaller group of dedicated followers, you can foster trust, credibility, and loyalty.

Think about it this way: if you had 10,000 followers but none of them were interested in your offerings or likely to become paying customers, what would be the point? On the other hand, if you have 500 followers who are genuinely interested in what you have to offer and are more likely to convert into customers, your efforts are much more likely to pay off.

Social selling is about leveraging social media to have real conversations and create meaningful connections. It's not just about broadcasting your message to the masses, but rather engaging in personalized interactions with individuals who have a genuine need for your products or services.

Remember, social selling is a long-term strategy that requires consistency and patience. It's not an overnight success formula, but rather a methodical approach to building trust and credibility with your target audience.

So how can you build your business through social selling without being a social media influencer? We'll explore that throughout this chapter.

Should I Do Social Selling?

Social selling may seem surreal or intimidating at first, especially if the idea of engaging with people on platforms like Facebook, LinkedIn, TikTok, Instagram, or X (formerly known as Twitter) feels overwhelming. However, as you dive into it and gain more experience, you might discover that it becomes an enjoyable and rewarding endeavor.

One of the main challenges people face with social selling is the feeling of talking to a screen instead of connecting with a real person. It can be difficult to gauge the impact of your actions, because many aspects of social selling are not easily measurable. For example, when you post on social media, you can see some statistics like the number of views, but you don't always know who those viewers are or the true impact your posts have on them. This lack of immediate and tangible results can be frustrating, especially in the early stages of social selling.

To put things into perspective, let's look at some current statistics. On average, it takes between six and ten touch points with a prospect on a social media platform for them to agree to have an offline conversation or a sales call. This means that social selling is a journey that requires persistence and consistency. In the beginning, you might invest a lot of effort without seeing immediate outcomes. It's a front-loaded process that will ultimately yield rewards later on. You need to be prepared for the long game and understand that it often takes multiple touch points to secure a meeting with a prospect.

So should you start social selling? Well, one crucial factor to consider is your willingness to dedicate time to social platforms. Social selling goes beyond simply posting and walking away. It's about actively building relationships on social media channels, and that requires consistent time and effort on your part.

Another essential aspect of social selling is content creation. By producing valuable content, you can educate and engage with your network, showcasing the value you bring. Content serves as a powerful tool for reaching and influencing a larger audience. However, creating content and engaging with those who respond to it, as well as actively reaching out to build your network, demand investment in terms of time and effort.

The beauty of social selling lies in its long-term benefits. Over time, as you consistently invest in your personal brand, content creation, and engagement, you build a platform. This platform becomes a testament to your expertise and reputation, working for you even when you're not actively promoting yourself. For example, my primary channel is LinkedIn, and over nearly a decade I have dedicated myself to building a presence on that platform. Now I receive daily inbound messages from people seeking my assistance. This level of visibility and reputation is a direct result of the ongoing investment I've made in building my network, creating content, and nurturing relationships on LinkedIn.

I believe that social selling is applicable to every business. So my answer is categorically *yes* and here are my reasons why:

- **Expanded Reach:** Social selling provides an unparalleled opportunity to reach a vast audience. Social media platforms have billions of active users, allowing you to connect with individuals from all around the world. By leveraging these platforms, you can expand your reach far beyond what traditional networking methods would allow.

- **Targeted Prospecting:** Social media platforms offer advanced targeting options that enable you to identify and engage with your ideal prospects. You can filter users based on demographics, interests, job titles, and more, ensuring that your efforts are focused on the individuals most likely to be interested in your products or services. This targeted prospecting saves time and resources by homing in on those who are genuinely interested in what you have to offer.

- **Relationship Building:** Social selling is all about building relationships. Social media platforms provide a unique environment where you can engage with prospects and customers on a more personal level. By consistently providing valuable content, engaging in conversations, and offering insights, you can establish trust and credibility, which are crucial for long-term business relationships.

- **Brand Awareness and Authority:** Through social selling, you have the opportunity to showcase your expertise and establish yourself as a thought leader in your industry. By consistently sharing valuable content, insights, and industry knowledge, you can position yourself as an authority figure. As your reputation grows, your brand awareness increases, making you the go-to resource for prospects seeking information or solutions in your niche.

- **Cost-Effective Marketing:** Social selling allows you to market your business at a fraction of the cost of traditional advertising methods. While paid advertising options exist on social media platforms, you can achieve significant results without spending a dime by focusing on organic reach. With compelling content and active engagement, you can capture the attention of your target audience without breaking the bank.

Social Selling: Without Becoming an Influencer

- **Increased Customer Insights:** Social media platforms provide valuable insights into your audience's preferences, interests, and behaviors. The analytics and data available allow you to gain a deeper understanding of your target market, helping you tailor your messaging, content, and offerings to better meet their needs. This valuable information can guide your overall marketing and sales strategies, leading to more effective campaigns and increased sales.

- **Competitive Advantage:** While social selling is becoming more popular, many businesses have yet to fully embrace its potential. By adopting social selling and leveraging it effectively, you can gain a competitive advantage over competitors who are slower to adapt. Social selling allows you to differentiate yourself, build stronger relationships, and capture the attention of prospects who may have overlooked traditional marketing approaches.

- **Access to Decision-Makers:** Social media platforms provide a direct line of communication with key decision-makers in companies. You can engage with executives, industry leaders, and influential individuals who may have been difficult to reach through traditional methods. By leveraging social selling, you can bypass gatekeepers and establish direct connections with those who have the power to make purchasing decisions.

- **Measurable Results:** While the immediate impact of social selling efforts may not always be visible, modern social media platforms provide valuable metrics and analytics. These insights allow you to measure the effectiveness of your social selling activities, track engagement levels, monitor conversions, and adjust your strategy accordingly. This data-driven approach ensures that your efforts are targeted, effective, and yielding measurable results.

Social selling has the potential to be a powerful strategy for your business. While it may feel unfamiliar or daunting at first, with dedication and consistency, you can unlock its benefits. Remember, social selling is not a quick fix or an overnight success story. It demands your time, effort, and a commitment to building relationships, creating valuable content, and establishing your personal brand. By investing in social selling, you position yourself to reap the rewards of a strong online presence, increased visibility, and the ability to attract and engage with prospects in a meaningful way.

Which Platforms Should I Use?

When it comes to choosing the right social media platforms for your social selling efforts, it's essential to avoid spreading yourself too thin. Many people fall into the trap of hopping around multiple platforms without achieving significant results. To make the most of your time and efforts, it's crucial to identify the one channel that will have the greatest impact on your business.

To determine which platform to focus on, consider the channel that provides the easiest access to your target decision-makers. In my case, I chose to go all in on LinkedIn because it allowed me to find and connect with the exact individuals who could help grow my business. By prioritizing the platform that provided the highest potential for reaching decision-makers, I was able to maximize my efforts and see tangible results.

My advice to you is to start with the one channel that offers the easiest access to your decision-makers from day one. By focusing your initial efforts on a specific platform, you can dedicate the necessary time and resources to make it work effectively. Once you have achieved success and established a solid presence on that platform, you can then consider expanding to other channels.

In my experience, while I had other social media channels like Facebook, TikTok, and YouTube, I shifted them into maintenance mode. I still posted on those platforms but didn't invest significant effort in actively building them out. My main focus was on LinkedIn, where I spent most of my time and energy.

For you, starting your social selling journey, the platform that works best may differ. It could be Facebook, Instagram, or another channel that aligns with your target audience and offers the easiest access to your decision-makers. The key is to identify that platform, make it work, and then gradually expand to other channels as you see fit.

Check out the platform's demographics. Websites such as pewresearch.org and sproutsocial.com regularly publish research on the demographics of the platforms. This can help you decide which platform is the best one for you.

Remember, it's crucial not to attempt to make every social media platform work simultaneously. By spreading your efforts across multiple platforms, you risk dividing your energy and diluting your impact. Instead, concentrate on one platform, invest in making it successful, and then consider adding additional channels to your strategy.

To sum it up, focus on identifying the social media platform that provides the easiest access to your decision-makers. Choose one channel, make it work, and build a strong presence there. As you establish success on that platform, you can gradually expand to other channels. This approach allows you to make the most of your efforts and achieve meaningful results in your social selling journey.

Where Do I Start?

Getting started with social selling on any channel requires focusing on key fundamental steps. Let's walk through the practical actions you need to take to be successful in your social selling journey.

Whether you choose Facebook, Instagram, LinkedIn, or any other platform, these steps will apply to your strategy.

Social selling is all about building and leveraging relationships to sell, rather than simply broadcasting or blindly pitching your services. We are bombarded with countless advertisements and sales pitches, so it's essential to take a more personalized and relationship-oriented approach to selling. Gone are the days when salespeople could rely solely on cold calls and generic mass emails. The modern buyer is more informed and discerning, and values authentic connections. Social selling allows you to tap into the power of social media platforms to establish meaningful relationships, build trust, and ultimately drive sales.

It's not a one-sided conversation. It's important to engage in two-way communication. Actively listen to your audience's feedback, respond to their comments, and address any concerns or inquiries they may have. This interaction helps to build trust and strengthens the relationship. Social selling also provides an excellent opportunity to network and connect with industry professionals, potential partners, and influencers. Join relevant groups and participate in discussions to expand your reach and foster valuable connections. By engaging with other professionals, you can tap into their networks and gain access to a wider audience.

The ultimate goal is to move the conversation offline and establish a more personal connection. Whether it's through a phone call, video chat, or in-person meeting, transitioning from online engagement to a more direct form of communication helps solidify the relationship and facilitates the sales process.

Here are the common elements to successful social selling:

1. **Optimize Your Profile:** The first step is to optimize your profile to attract your ideal clients, your most valuable clients. Take the time to carefully craft your "About" section,

banner, or bio. Ensure that it clearly articulates the value you offer and speaks directly to your target audience. Utilize your big promise statement across your social profile to convey the key benefits you provide. Additionally, incorporate relevant keywords in your profile description to enhance discoverability. By doing so, people searching for specific terms related to your offerings will find you more easily. Remember, use your big promise statement to demonstrate the value you provide quickly and clearly.

2. **Produce Valuable Content:** Content creation is a crucial aspect of social selling. Develop a content schedule that allows you to consistently share valuable content with your audience. This content should strike a balance between information about yourself, your offerings, and content that genuinely helps your target audience, your most valuable clients. Avoid solely self-promoting as it will likely generate little interest. Instead, focus on answering the question "What's in it for them?" Tailor your content to provide value and address the needs of your audience. Share insights, tips, industry news, and other relevant information that can help your audience overcome challenges or achieve their goals. By doing so, you'll establish yourself as a trusted resource and build credibility.

3. **Grow Your Following:** To expand your reach and results of your social selling efforts, you need to grow your following or connections on the chosen social media platform. The approach may differ depending on the platform you choose. Platforms like Instagram, X, and TikTok require attracting people to follow you by creating engaging content and utilizing relevant hashtags. On the other hand, platforms like LinkedIn and Facebook allow you to proactively connect or

send friend requests to build your network. Focus on expanding your pool of connections or followers by reaching out to individuals who align with your target audience and have the potential to become valuable prospects. Engage with their content, leave thoughtful comments, and start conversations. By building genuine connections and showing a sincere interest in their work or opinions, you'll establish a foundation for fruitful relationships.

4. **Engage Your Prospects:** Engaging with your connections and followers is critical for building relationships and moving prospects along the buyer's journey. Remember, it typically takes around six to ten touch points to get someone to agree to an offline conversation or sales call. Engage with your audience regularly by interacting with their content, leaving thoughtful comments, and sending direct messages. Show genuine interest in their work, ask questions, and provide valuable insights or suggestions. Invest time and effort in building relationships, because this will increase the likelihood of prospects being open to having a conversation with you. Consistently allocate part of your day to engaging with these individuals and making the ask for a conversation. Personalize your messages and demonstrate that you've taken the time to understand their needs and challenges. By doing so, you'll stand out from the crowd and establish yourself as a trusted advisor.

Here's a helpful tip: If you engage with your prospects consistently every day and make conversation requests regularly, you will start receiving responses and calls. It's a matter of putting in the time and effort to generate the desired results. Remember, social selling is a long-term strategy, so be patient and persistent.

Consistency is key. Dedicate time each day to social selling activities, whether it's creating and scheduling content, engaging with your audience, or reaching out to prospects. Monitor your progress, measure the effectiveness of your efforts, and adjust as needed. Remember, social selling requires consistent effort and dedication, but the rewards in terms of expanded reach, relationship-building, and business growth are well worth it.

Successful social selling starts with optimizing your profile, producing valuable content, growing your following, and engaging with your prospects. By following these practical steps, you'll establish a strong presence on your chosen social media platform, connect with your target audience, and generate meaningful business opportunities. Social selling is about building relationships, providing value, and positioning yourself as a trusted resource. Embrace the journey, be authentic, and adapt your strategy based on the needs and preferences of your audience.

With dedication and persistence, social selling can become a powerful tool in your sales and marketing arsenal. Social selling has the potential to generate significant revenue and contribute to your business's success. I have a client whose primary focus is LinkedIn. They spend approximately two to three hours per week on the platform, consistently sharing posts, engaging with prospects, and initiating offline conversations. In just six months, they have generated nearly $5 million in sales through their social selling efforts on LinkedIn. This result underscores the fundamental principle of sales success: talking to more of the right people.

The beauty of social selling is that there are no real limits on the potential earnings. As you engage in social selling and build relationships, you have the opportunity to expand your team. For instance, you can hire more social sellers to further leverage social media platforms and increase your reach. By scaling your efforts and effectively managing your team, you can expand your business and tap into more revenue streams.

The key factor that determines your success in social selling is your commitment to the plan. The more time and effort you dedicate to talking to the right people, the greater your potential for generating revenue. Social selling allows you to have prolific interactions with prospects, expanding your network and increasing the number of valuable conversations you can have.

In essence, social selling is a powerful strategy to engage with more prospects and get in front of a broader audience. Your earnings potential is directly linked to the amount of time you can devote to connecting with the right people. The limit is not defined by any external factors but rather by the amount of time you can invest in social selling activities.

The Seven Steps of Social Selling

It's essential to approach social selling with a strategic mindset, avoiding aggressive or overtly promotional tactics. Instead, focus on building genuine relationships and engaging with potential prospects in a meaningful way.

One effective approach to social selling is what I refer to as the "seven steps," a model designed to create touchpoints with prospects over time, ultimately building awareness, trust, and relationships. By incorporating these seven steps into your social selling strategy, you can establish authentic connections with potential clients and position yourself as a trusted resource.

Over a period of a few weeks you build relationships by engaging your prospects on a social media platform. Instead of diving in head first and pitching your services, you invest time to let them see your content and deliberately engage with them (with no expectation of selling anything) to break the ice and build a relationship. Remember, people buy from people they know, like, and trust. You can't do that with one message, one like, one comment or post.

109

1. Engage with their Content Meaningfully

Start by identifying potential prospects on social media platforms and engaging with their content. Like, comment on, and share their posts to show genuine interest in their perspectives and insights. This initial step helps you get on their radar and indicates that you're an active participant in their online community.

This isn't just a "great post" comment—you need to actively engage in meaningful discussions.

2. Follow, Connect, and Friend

Once you've engaged with their content, take the next step by following, connecting, or friending them on the respective social media platform. This action not only shows your continued interest but also increases the likelihood of further engagement and interaction.

3. The Thank You/Complimentary Message

After connecting, send a personalized message thanking them for accepting your connection or follow request. Express appreciation for their content and, if relevant, mention any specific posts or insights that resonated with you. Keep the message friendly, sincere, and devoid of any sales pitch. One of the best ways to do this is to briefly introduce yourself and give them a complimentary note. This will help differentiate you from all the annoying messages they get from people.

Remember, it's important you show you've done your homework; don't let your engagement with prospects look generic or robotic. Make it personal and human.

4. Engage with Their Content

Maintain an active presence on their profile by regularly engaging with their posts. Share insightful comments and participate in discussions, showcasing your expertise without being overly self-promotional. This ongoing engagement helps nurture the relationship and establish you as a valuable member of their network.

5. Break the Ice with Relevant Discussions

One of the first rules of outreach is to work to get a response. While we can't invest time engaging prospects who don't respond, many prospects ignore or don't respond because people just pitch them or are not prepared to do a little bit of groundwork.

Starting a conversation in the DMs about something relevant to their posts or on topics they may have an interest in can help prompt people to engage and respond. Doing this icebreaking stage will increase the number of positive responses in the future.

One of the simplest methods is to complement them on something relevant that is going on in their company or business. Then simply follow up and ask a question about it. Genuinely show interest.

6. Content-Rich Direct Messages

As you deepen the connection, begin sending content-rich direct messages (DMs) tailored to their interests and needs. Share articles, videos, or resources that could benefit them. Keep these messages informative and non-salesy, focusing on providing value rather than pitching your services. These could be articles or blogs that speak to the pain points and desired outcomes of your prospect.

I sometimes create blogs meant specifically to share with prospects in the messages, in order to speak to their needs and reference my own experiences from working with clients. This is a soft way to sell and introduce how I help people in a focused but more informative way.

7. Send an Outreach Message

After interacting with their profile six times, it's time to send an outreach message. Frame the message as a natural continuation of your previous interactions, expressing your genuine desire to help and explore potential collaboration. Highlight any specific areas where you believe your expertise could be beneficial to them.

In your outreach message, offer the opportunity to schedule a discovery call to discuss their needs and goals in more detail. With the trust you've built through the previous six steps, you're more likely to receive a positive response and engage in a productive conversation.

If you've been following the steps, your prospect will have likely checked out your profile a few times and so your profile and personal brand will have helped educate them. Messages don't need to be long winded, complex, or waffly if you focus on being relevant and relational.

By following these seven steps over a few-week period, you'll effectively build your relationship with potential prospects, culminating in the final touchpoint of a personalized outreach message and offer of a discovery call. This gradual approach puts trust-building at the forefront, leading to better responses to DMs and smoother discovery calls.

One of the key advantages of this process is that prospects will often visit your profile and content multiple times throughout the engagement. As a result, you'll have additional opportunities to educate and inform them about your expertise and offerings. By showcasing valuable content on your profile, you further solidify your position as a trusted resource.

Customizing Your Strategy for Each Platform

In the following sections, we'll explore some tips for specific platforms that will help you customize your strategy.

LinkedIn

LinkedIn provides a valuable platform for social selling, and you can leverage its search features to find your target audience. The advanced search functionality allows you to narrow down your search based on various criteria such as industry, job title, location, and more. By using these search features effectively, you can identify individuals who align with your ideal client profile and have a higher likelihood of being interested in your offerings.

Once you have identified potential prospects, it's essential to engage with their content before sending connection requests. This step is crucial for building a genuine connection and establishing familiarity. Take the time to read their posts, articles, and comments, and leave thoughtful and relevant responses. Engaging with their content showcases your interest and demonstrates that you are not simply seeking a transactional connection, but genuinely value their insights and perspectives.

When engaging with their content, be sure to add value to the conversation. Share your expertise, provide additional insights, or ask meaningful questions that prompt further discussion. This approach shows that you have taken the time to understand their content and are interested in meaningful engagement. It helps to position you as a knowledgeable and credible professional in your field.

By engaging with their content first, you increase the chances of your connection request being accepted. When sending the connection request, personalize the message and reference the interaction you had with their content. This personalized approach demonstrates that you are intentional in your outreach and have a genuine interest in connecting.

Facebook

Facebook offers a valuable opportunity for social selling, and one effective strategy is to join interest groups where your target audience congregates. These groups are often focused on specific topics, industries, or shared interests, making them ideal environments to engage with potential prospects. By joining relevant interest groups, you gain access to a concentrated community of individuals who are likely to be interested in your offerings.

Once you've joined these interest groups, the key is to actively engage in discussions and provide value to the community. Take the time to understand the dynamics of the group and the types of conversations taking place. This will allow you to contribute meaningfully to the discussions and position yourself as a valuable participant.

When engaging in discussions, focus on providing insights, answering questions, and offering helpful advice. By sharing your expertise, you establish credibility and demonstrate your value to the group members. Actively participate in conversations, listen to others' perspectives, and be respectful in your interactions.

As you engage in these discussions, pay attention to individuals who consistently contribute or show interest in similar topics. These individuals are likely to have aligned interests and may be potential prospects for your business. Once you've identified these individuals, it's appropriate to send them friend requests.

When sending friend requests, be sure to personalize your message and reference the shared discussion or topic. This demonstrates that you have taken the time to engage with their content and have a genuine interest in connecting. The personalized approach sets you apart from generic connection requests and increases the chances of your request being accepted.

As you build your network through these interest groups, continue engaging with your connections by liking, commenting, and sharing their posts. This ongoing engagement helps to maintain the relationship, stay visible in their feeds, and nurture connections over time. By consistently demonstrating your interest and support, you strengthen the bond and increase the likelihood of potential business opportunities.

X

This is a powerful platform for social selling, and one effective strategy is to find high-profile accounts that are likely to have your target audience as followers. These high-profile accounts often have a significant reach and a dedicated following that aligns with your ideal customer profile. By engaging with these accounts and participating in discussions around their tweets, you can tap into their audience and increase your visibility among potential prospects.

Start by identifying high-profile accounts that cater to your target audience. Look for thought leaders, industry influencers, or businesses that share similar interests or cater to the same market segment as your business. These accounts often have a substantial following and active engagement on their tweets.

Once you've identified these high-profile accounts, focus on sharing insights and valuable contributions in the discussions surrounding their tweets. Reply to their tweets with thoughtful and relevant comments that add value to the conversation. By showcasing your expertise and providing valuable insights, you position yourself as a knowledgeable and credible professional in your industry.

As you engage in discussions, pay attention to individuals who actively participate or show interest in similar topics. These individuals are likely to be potential prospects for your business. Take the initiative to follow them on X and continue engaging with their tweets.

When following potential prospects, it's important to engage with their content regularly. Like and retweet their tweets and reply to their posts with meaningful comments. This level of engagement shows that you are genuinely interested in their insights and opinions. It helps to establish a connection and foster familiarity with your target audience.

In addition to engaging with individual tweets, you can also join relevant X chats and participate in industry-specific conversations. X chats are organized discussions around a specific hashtag, allowing individuals with similar interests to connect and engage. By actively participating in these chats, you expand your reach and network within your industry.

TikTok

TikTok has emerged as a popular platform for social selling, and one effective strategy is to research high-performing videos in your niche. By analyzing these successful videos, you can gain insights into what resonates with your target audience and how you can create similar content from your own unique perspective.

To begin, spend time exploring TikTok and identify videos that have gained significant traction within your niche. Look for videos that have garnered a high number of views, likes, comments, and shares. These metrics indicate that the content has resonated with the audience and has the potential to engage and captivate viewers.

As you research these high-performing videos, pay attention to the key elements that contribute to their success. Pay attention to the content, style, format, hashtags, and storytelling techniques employed in these videos. Consider the emotions evoked, the humor used, or the educational value they provide. This analysis will help you identify patterns and strategies that can be adapted to create your own compelling content.

While it's essential to draw inspiration from these high-performing videos, it's equally important to infuse your unique perspective and voice into your content. Think about how you can add value and differentiate yourself from others in your niche. What expertise or insights can you bring to the table? How can you provide a fresh take or a unique angle that resonates with your target audience?

Once you have a clear understanding of the successful videos and have identified the elements you want to incorporate, it's time to create your own content. Leverage TikTok's creative tools, such as filters, effects, and soundtracks, to enhance the visual appeal and engagement of your videos.

Instagram

The Instagram platform has provided Instagram Reels, which has quickly become a powerful tool for social selling, and leveraging this feature can help you grow your following at an accelerated pace. By creating short and useful Reels that resonate with your audience, you can attract new followers and increase your visibility on the platform. Additionally, incorporating trending sounds in your Reels can aid in their discovery by a wider audience.

Instagram Reels allows you to create 5-second to 90-second videos that can be entertaining, informative, or both. They provide a dynamic and visually appealing format to engage your audience and showcase your expertise. To boost the potential of Reels for social selling, it's crucial to focus on creating content that is relevant, valuable, and aligned with your target audience's interests.

When creating Reels, consider the pain points or challenges your audience faces and provide practical solutions or tips in your videos. This can be done through step-by-step demonstrations, quick tutorials, or sharing bite-sized nuggets of information. By offering valuable content, you position yourself as a trusted resource and attract followers who find your content helpful and engaging.

To further enhance the visibility and reach of your Reels, it's important to incorporate trending sounds. Instagram's algorithm often promotes Reels that feature popular sounds or audio clips.

By using trending sounds, you increase the likelihood of your Reels being discovered by a broader audience and potentially going viral.

Stay up to date with the latest trends and explore the Reels section on Instagram to identify popular sounds that are relevant to your niche. Consider how you can incorporate these sounds into your content in a creative and meaningful way. This can be through lip-syncing, voiceovers, or utilizing the sound as a backdrop to complement your visuals.

Consistency is key when it comes to Instagram Reels. Aim to post regularly and establish a predictable content schedule. This helps your audience anticipate and engage with your content consistently, increasing their loyalty and likelihood of sharing your Reels with their own followers.

Chapter 8

Creating Prolific Content Efficiently and Effectively

Creating content is indeed a crucial aspect of social selling and building a successful online presence. By prolifically producing content, you can expand your reach, engage with a wider audience, and establish yourself as a thought leader in your industry. This principle applies not only to social media platforms but also to your website and other online channels.

Content is often referred to as the king of digital marketing because it forms the foundation of your online presence. It allows you to share valuable insights, expertise, and information with your target audience, establishing credibility and trust. Moreover, it provides an avenue to showcase your unique perspectives and differentiate yourself from competitors.

When it comes to social selling, creating content that aligns with your audience's interests and pain points is essential. It allows you to address their challenges, provide solutions, and offer guidance that positions you as a valuable resource. By consistently producing relevant and valuable content, you increase your chances of attracting potential customers and nurturing relationships with existing ones.

Your website is a powerful platform to publish and showcase your content. Having a well-designed website with a dedicated blog section enables you to create long-form articles, guides, case studies, and other forms of valuable content. This content not only educates and engages your audience but also serves as a magnet for organic search traffic, increasing your online visibility and attracting potential customers who are actively seeking information.

Creating content beyond social media and your website can further amplify your reach. Consider exploring guest blogging opportunities, where you can contribute content to other reputable websites in your industry. This exposes your expertise to new audiences and provides valuable backlinks to your own website, improving your search engine optimization (SEO) and credibility.

Podcasting is another powerful content creation avenue that allows you to share your knowledge and engage with your audience in an audio format. By hosting a podcast, you can invite industry experts, conduct interviews, and share valuable insights on various topics. This medium provides an intimate and convenient way for your audience to consume content, expanding your reach and establishing authority within your niche.

It's crucial to note that while quantity is important, maintaining the quality of your content should not be overlooked. Ensure that your content is well-researched and well-written, and provides genuine value to your audience. This will help build trust and credibility, fostering long-term relationships with your followers and potential customers.

The Big Challenge of Creating Content

Content creation has become an integral part of our digital lives, from blog posts and social media updates to videos and podcasts. While the demand for fresh content is ever-increasing, many individuals find it challenging to consistently produce engaging and unique material. There are three primary reasons why people struggle to consistently create content: the constant battle for fresh ideas, the fear of repetition, and the elusive pursuit of time.

1. Struggling for Ideas

One of the most common roadblocks content creators encounter is the lack of fresh and compelling ideas. The pressure to deliver original and valuable content can be overwhelming, leading to creative paralysis. Generating new ideas requires a combination of inspiration, research, and a deep understanding of the audience.

Content creators often find themselves facing the dreaded creative block, where their minds go blank and ideas seem to evaporate. The fear of producing subpar content or being unoriginal can hinder their ability to come up with fresh ideas. With billions of pieces of content circulating on the internet, finding a unique angle or topic can be challenging. The fear of repeating what has already been said can discourage creators from even starting.

Riding the wave of trends can generate significant traffic and engagement. However, constantly chasing trends can be exhausting and may not align with a creator's true passion or expertise. This dilemma often leaves content creators torn between creating what's popular and creating what truly resonates with them.

2. Feeling Like They're Saying the Same Thing

Another obstacle content creators face is the fear of sounding repetitive or redundant. They worry that their content will become monotonous, leading to disengagement from their audience. This fear can stem from various factors, including:

- In some niches or industries, the scope of content topics may be relatively narrow. Creators may feel trapped within the confines of their niche, struggling to find new angles to approach familiar subjects. Content creators often draw from their own experiences and expertise to produce meaningful content. However, over time, it can become challenging to find new perspectives or fresh insights, making them feel like they are saying the same things repeatedly.

- If a particular type of content or topic has been successful in the past, creators may feel compelled to replicate it continuously. However, the fear of becoming one-dimensional or losing their creative spark can deter them from revisiting similar ideas.

3. Not Finding the Time to Create

Time is a finite resource, and content creation requires a significant investment of it. Many individuals struggle to find the necessary time to create content consistently due to various reasons, such as:

- Content creation often competes with numerous other responsibilities and commitments, such as work, family, and personal obligations. Balancing these aspects of life can leave little time and energy for consistent content creation.
- Creating high-quality content involves not only the creation itself but also researching, editing, and promoting it. This multifaceted process can quickly become overwhelming, especially for individuals who manage all aspects of their content creation independently.

The pursuit of perfection can be a double-edged sword. While striving for excellence is admirable, it can also lead to a never-ending quest for flawlessness. The constant need to refine and perfect content can consume an excessive amount of time, preventing creators from consistently producing new material.

Consistently creating content is no small feat.

Overcoming the Content Creation Problem

The key to overcoming the obstacles described in the previous section lies in establishing a structured approach that revolves around understanding the motivations of your most valuable clients (MVCs), defining topics, and breaking down knowledge into bite-sized chunks. Chapter 2, "Knowing Your Most Valuable Clients," already discussed your MVCs, so here we're going to focus on defining and understanding topics. We'll begin with separating macro content from micro content.

Macro content refers to high-level subtopics that encompass broad subjects, such as "how to get leads from LinkedIn" or "how to build a business online." These subtopics are extensive and contain a wealth of information that could potentially fill entire books. However, many content creators make the mistake of considering their work on macro topics as comprehensive, when in reality they have only touched the surface. Macro content can take various forms, such as blog posts, podcasts, PDF guides, or videos.

On the other hand, micro content involves breaking down macro topics into their constituent elements and offering valuable insights at a more detailed level. For instance, within the macro topic of "how to build a business online," subtopics like building a social media profile, creating content, or utilizing hashtags can be explored. Micro content can delve even deeper, covering specific aspects like the best time to send a direct message (DM) on LinkedIn. Micro content provides readers with tiny, easily digestible nuggets of information that are explained thoroughly and concisely.

To tackle the content creation problem, it is crucial to break down knowledge systematically. This process begins by categorizing topics and listing out macro and micro content. By organizing

Creating Prolific Content Efficiently and Effectively

ideas into clear categories, you can avoid the daunting task of deciding what to post or write about each day. Documenting ideas in a Google Doc or note-taking app ensures that they are captured even when they occur unexpectedly, such as during walks or other activities. This practice prevents valuable content ideas from slipping away and helps build a repository of potential topics.

One common challenge faced by content creators is the phenomenon known as "blank page paralysis." When sitting down to write, it is not uncommon for all the knowledge and ideas to evaporate into thin air, leaving you at a loss for words. However, by adopting a structured approach and referring to the documented list of topics, you'll alleviate this paralysis. Having a clear outline of macro and micro content ideas allows for a smoother flow of ideas and facilitates the process of creating valuable content. (See Table 8.1.)

Content creators often underestimate the value of sharing basic information. What may seem obvious or mundane to an expert can

Table 8.1 Macro and micro content examples.

Topic	Macro	Micro
Growing a business online	Which social media channel is the best?	Instagram reels versus TikTok: which is easier to create?
Job hunting	How to apply for a job	Six things a recruiter is looking for on your CV
Life coaching	How to get the most from life coaching	Five questions to ask a life coach before you hire them
Financial planning for retirement	Saving for retirement	Will $1,000,000 be enough to retire?

be a mystery to someone with less knowledge or experience. Therefore, you should seize the opportunity to explain even the most fundamental concepts. By sharing insights that might be taken for granted, you can provide valuable guidance to your audience. It is essential to remember that your content is intended for those who are not as far along in their journey or do not possess the same level of expertise as you have.

You may feel the need to provide more comprehensive or advanced information, as you'll view your content from your expert standpoint. However, it is crucial to remember that content is primarily meant to benefit others who are seeking guidance. By reframing the perspective and recognizing that the content is for individuals with varying levels of knowledge, you'll avoid the trap of perfectionism or worse, creating content for experts like you, which will fly over the heads of your audience. Sharing basic information and explaining concepts that seem obvious to the creator can be valuable to your target audience.

To generate a steady stream of macro and micro content ideas, content creators can employ the following strategies:

- Keep a running list of content ideas and categorize them into macro and micro topics. This ensures that valuable ideas are captured and readily available for content creation.

- Overcoming the content creation problem requires a structured approach that involves breaking down knowledge into macro and micro content. While macro content covers high-level topics, micro content delves into the finer details, providing readers with valuable insights.

- By organizing your ideas, documenting them, and recognizing the importance of sharing macro and micro content, you'll never run out of ideas.

In the ever-evolving landscape of content creation, finding new and innovative ways to engage your audience is crucial. One effective strategy is to repurpose existing content and present it from a fresh or different perspective. By doing so, you can extend the lifespan of your content, reach new audiences, and reinforce key messages. This chapter delves into the art of repurposing content, provides practical tips for giving a new slant to the same underlying ideas, and highlights the benefits of this approach.

The Power of Repurposing Content

You might feel like saying the same thing over and over again is bad. It isn't. It means you have focus and you are sticking to your topics. It's actually a good thing to be repurposing your content.

Repurposing content involves taking existing ideas, concepts, or messages and presenting them in alternative formats or through different channels. Rather than reinventing the wheel for every piece of content, repurposing allows you to leverage the value of your existing work while maximizing its reach and impact. This strategy not only saves time and resources but also enables you to adapt your content to suit diverse platforms and cater to varied audience preferences.

The benefit of repurposing content is that you can say the same thing in different ways. You can refine and build upon what you've already done and reduce the amount of time you spend making 100% new content. Instead of starting from scratch, you can build upon existing ideas, saving time and effort. This efficiency enables you to consistently deliver valuable content without sacrificing quality. Presenting the same underlying idea from different angles reinforces your core message. By providing diverse perspectives, you can emphasize key points, making them more memorable and impactful for your audience.

Strategies for Repurposing Content with a Fresh Perspective

There are a number of ways to jumpstart your approach to repurposing content and breathe new life into your content:

- **Identify Core Ideas:** Begin by identifying the fundamental ideas, concepts, or messages within your existing content. These core ideas serve as the foundation for creating fresh perspectives.

- **Analyze Audience Preferences:** Understand your target audience's preferences, interests, and preferred content formats. This analysis helps determine the most effective ways to repurpose your content and tailor it to different platforms.

- **Dive Deeper:** Take a deep dive into a specific aspect of your original content and explore it in more detail. This approach allows you to provide in-depth insights, share case studies, or offer step-by-step guides that expand upon the original idea. Drill down and take one point from a previous post and expand it.

- **Offer a Contrasting Perspective:** Present a fresh slant by offering a contrasting viewpoint or addressing common misconceptions related to your core idea. This approach sparks curiosity and engages readers who may have encountered similar content in the past.

- **Provide Case Studies or Examples:** Support your core idea with real-world examples or case studies that illustrate its application or success. This strategy adds credibility and helps readers connect with your content on a practical level.

- **Collaborate with Others:** Invite industry experts or influencers to contribute their perspectives on the same underlying idea. This collaborative approach not only adds diversity to your content but also exposes your audience to different viewpoints and expands your network.

- **Make the Content Specific to a Situation:** Adapting existing content for specific situations or scenarios your audience may face can be a great way to adapt your content and make it unique and more relevant. For example, turn a post into a more micro piece applicable to a situation or problem the audience may face.

- **Leverage User-Generated Content:** Encourage your audience to contribute their experiences, opinions, or interpretations related to your core idea. This user-generated content can serve as a valuable resource for creating fresh perspectives and fostering a sense of community.

Repurposing Other People's Ideas

Getting inspiration from others is a common practice. You may think, "Everything has already been said online, so why do I need to say it?" You need to say it because your take will be different. You may disagree with someone else's content, or you may see it from a different angle. You may have different experiences to share.

So even if it has been said, nobody has said it like you will.

Researching what content others have made allows you to explore different perspectives, gain insights, and identify trends. However, replicating existing ideas is plagiarism. You need to use their idea and make it your own. Researching what content already exists and using that to make your own version will give millions of ideas.

Here are the benefits of using existing content as inspiration:

- **Broadened Perspectives:** Researching existing content exposes you to a wide range of ideas, opinions, and perspectives.

It expands your knowledge base and helps you understand the content landscape within your niche.

- **Idea Generation:** Studying content created by others can spark fresh ideas and creative thinking. It allows you to identify gaps or opportunities that you can leverage to develop your unique content.

- **Validation of Concepts:** Content research enables you to validate the viability and relevance of certain topics or ideas. By observing the engagement, reception, and success of existing content, you can gauge the potential interest in similar topics.

- **Improving Existing Ideas:** Studying others' content can inspire you to enhance or build upon existing ideas. By examining what has already been done, you can identify areas where you can provide additional value or a fresh perspective.

It's important before you start that you clearly define your content goals and the purpose behind your research. Determine what specific aspects or themes you want to explore and how they align with your target audience's interests. How do you research? Look for respected influencers, thought leaders, and established brands within your niche. Analyze their content to gain insights into successful strategies, trending topics, and popular formats. Explore content that has significant engagement, such as high views, likes, comments, or shares. Also look at the top-performing content on YouTube or in web searches. Identify the elements that make these pieces successful, including writing style, format, visuals, or unique angles.

Look for areas where existing content is lacking or where you believe you can provide a fresh perspective. Consider the unanswered questions—what did they not share in the original content? Is this an opportunity for you? Join forums like Reddit and Quora to see what discussions and questions come up often.

Adding Your Unique Spin

Once you have conducted thorough research, identify how you can contribute a fresh perspective to the existing conversations. Find unique angles, challenge conventional wisdom, or present a different point of view. Include personal stories, anecdotes, or case studies that relate to the topic at hand. Sharing your own insights and experiences adds authenticity and establishes a deeper connection with your audience. Take the information you have gathered and distil it into practical advice or actionable steps. Offer tangible solutions, tips, or strategies that your audience can implement to achieve their goals. Use storytelling techniques to captivate your audience. Weave narratives, use vivid descriptions, and create relatable scenarios to engage readers on an emotional level. Infuse your content with your authentic voice and personality. Develop a distinct brand voice that resonates with your target audience, allowing them to connect with your unique style.

Replaying Your Best Hits

So you've created a piece of content. Maybe it's a blog post, a video, or a social media update. You've shared it with the world, but what happens next? Do you just let it fade into the depths of the internet, never to be seen again? Often we make a piece of content and never fully utilize the key points we make. We might create a short video and share it on social media, only for it never to see the light of day again.

This is a mistake. We often overlook the value of reposting our best-performing content. We pour time and effort into creating something amazing, but we fail to fully leverage its potential. Instead, we should look to replay our greatest hits.

Think about the music industry. They make a fortune from people listening to the same songs over and over again. They make money from producing music that is replayed all around the world. Some people will be hearing the song for the first time even though it's being played on the radio four or five times a day; others will hear it two or three times a day.

Reposting content that has performed well is not lazy—it's smart. You are squeezing every bit of value you can out of the content you've made.

We may feel like it's bad to repost old content because we figure people have already seen it. But in reality only a tiny percentage of people will have seen the content and remember it. Because it was something you created, you know it intimately, but your audience may have just vaguely seen it. Using a piece of content only once is a massive waste of your effort. Remember, you should be replaying the best-performing pieces.

When you make a piece of content, if you want to replay your best hits it's important that you track your metrics. This helps you know what works and what doesn't, and enables you to create a list of content you want to replay. It also helps you improve your content based on what is high-performing and what isn't. Over time, tracking your metrics will teach you to produce better content.

I recommend reposting your best hits every six to eight weeks. You don't need to repost everything, but a third of your content could be replayed hits. This method of reusing content has the benefit of increasing your baseline, reducing your content creation time, and extracting the maximum ROI from your content creation time.

Within a few months of posting consistently, you'll have a back catalogue of content you can reuse.

Reformatting Your Content

This will allow you to rapidly scale your output of content without increasing your work. It's such a simple thing, yet very few people do it.

Every time I create a post for social media, I also convert it into a video and a blog. They may be short blogs and short videos, but it means I've turned the same content into different formats.

If you make a video, why not turn it into a single image or a flippable carousel of images and use the idea again? Different people consume content in different ways, so some may have missed the video, but the carousel will be engaging for others. Switch up the medium, using different media to get your points across.

Here are some examples.

- Turn a still image post into a carousel.
- Turn a carousel into a video.
- Turn a video into a blog.
- Turn a blog into a podcast.

Every piece of content can be turned into another format. I often start with my LinkedIn posts. From those I create a carousel, blog, and video. In essence my posts expand and become more detailed blogs and videos.

Why keep making new content when you can reformat what you've already created? It makes sense to reformat your content; it's quicker to turn something you've already made into a different format than come up with something new.

Content Tips for Driving More Engagement

We've examined a lot of ways to approach creating content and make it meaningful for your audience. But there is still more you can do to make your content truly connect with people and drive engagement even further:

- **Start with a Captivating Introduction:** Hook your readers from the beginning with an engaging introduction that clearly states the purpose of your content and entices them to continue reading.

- **Use a Conversational Tone:** Write in a conversational style that feels approachable and friendly. Avoid overly intellectual or formal language unless it's necessary for your target audience.

- **Striking Visuals:** One of the most critical elements of success with your social content and blogs is having visuals that compel people to stop scrolling and start reading. Use clear, bold statements and engaging visuals to attract people, helping to stop them from scrolling past and getting them to read more.

- **Keep It Concise:** In the age of information overload, it's important to keep your content concise and to the point. Remove any unnecessary fluff and ensure that every sentence contributes to the overall message.

- **Avoid Jargon:** Filling your content with acronyms and jargon will confuse the audience. Keep your writing simple and easy to follow.

- **Use Emojis and Bullet Points:** Break up your content into sections. This helps readers skim through the content and find the specific information they're looking for. Use emojis and bullet points to present lists or key points in a clear and concise manner.

- **Provide Actionable Takeaways:** Make your content practical and actionable by including clear takeaways or steps that readers can implement. This adds value to your content and encourages readers to engage with it.

- **Incorporate Storytelling Techniques:** Weave storytelling elements into your content to make it more relatable and memorable. Share anecdotes, personal experiences, or case studies that help illustrate your points and connect with your audience emotionally.

- **Use Examples and Visuals:** Support your content with relevant examples, case studies, or visuals. This helps clarify complex concepts and makes your content more engaging and memorable.

- **Edit and Proofread:** Always proofread your content before publishing. Check for grammar and spelling errors, ensure proper formatting, and review the overall flow and coherence of your content. Consider using editing tools or seeking feedback from others to catch any mistakes or improve the quality of your writing.

- **Inject Your Personality:** Don't be afraid to let your personality shine through in your content. Injecting your unique voice and perspective adds authenticity and makes your content more engaging.

- **Incorporate Data and Statistics:** Support your claims and arguments with data and statistics from reputable sources. This adds credibility to your content and makes it more informative. Numbers in content and titles get lots of attention.

- **Use Relevant and Relatable Examples:** Use examples that your audience can easily relate to. This helps them understand the concepts you're discussing and see how it applies to their own lives or situations.

- **Use Hashtags:** Most platforms rely on hashtags to help people find your content. Ensure you use 3–10 hashtags on your posts on social media to help it be found by more people.

- **Optimize for Dwell Time:** As a general rule, you want your content in whatever format to hold the attention of the audience. In the world of social media, holding the attention of a user for 30–60 seconds will get you a lot of reach and visibility. It's not just about longer videos, blogs, or posts; it's about holding attention.

Chapter 9

Unleashing Your Selling and Marketing Power with Email

Isn't email dead?

Actually, no. Email is not only alive and well, it's crucial. As I'm writing, email is still one of the best marketing channels with the highest ROI. While we have social media and paid advertising, there is nothing more powerful to a business than being able to reach their customers on demand.

I've built my business on the back of email and social media. In 2018, I launched a series of workshops for businesses. I used email to fill them. I didn't spend any money on ads; I just used marketing lists to promote my events. Over the course of two years, more than 5,000 people came to those events and I made more than $500,000 doing it. All that from email marketing.

The only reason I stopped was the Covid pandemic.

Email is powerful. Yes it's noisy and you have to work harder than ever to make it successful, but what isn't noisy these days?

Email isn't dead, and building an email list is absolutely essential if you want long-term growth in your business.

Why You Need an Email List

For small businesses striving to make their mark in the competitive market, an email list can be a game-changer. While social media platforms

135

and other digital marketing techniques are essential, building and maintaining an email list holds significant value. An email list provides small businesses with a direct and personalized channel of communication with their target audience. Unlike social media platforms where algorithms dictate the visibility of your content, emails allow you to reach subscribers' inboxes directly. By collecting email addresses of interested prospects or customers, small businesses can ensure that their messages are delivered directly to the intended recipients.

Understanding the Customer Buying Journey

Understanding the customer buying journey is essential to comprehend why not all customers are ready to buy at a given moment. The buying journey typically consists of several stages:

1. Awareness
2. Consideration
3. Evaluation
4. Purchase
5. Post-purchase

Each customer progresses through these stages at their own pace, influenced by various factors such as their needs, preferences, budget, and level of trust in the brand.

At the awareness stage, customers become aware of a problem or need they have. In the consideration stage, they start examining their needs and researching potential solutions. During the evaluation stage, they compare and assess the different options that are available. It is during these early stages that customers may not be ready to make a purchase. They are gathering information, seeking advice, and comparing alternatives.

Regular email communication is a powerful tool for nurturing leads by addressing their pain points, answering their questions, and providing solutions. By consistently delivering valuable content, such as newsletters, case studies, educational resources, or industry insights, your business can establish credibility, demonstrate your expertise, and position you as a trusted advisor. This process is crucial through the awareness, consideration, and evaluation stages of the customer buying journey, helping potential buyers develop trust in the brand, fostering a sense of confidence that can eventually lead to a purchase decision. It's also important at the post-purchase stage, because it shows your investment in continuing to build your relationship with your customer and address their needs, which can lead to future purchases.

Using Your Email List in the Customer Buying Journey

Now that you're grounded in the customer buying journey's stages of awareness, consideration, evaluation, purchase, and post-purchase, you're ready to explore how your email list can work with it to build your customer relationships. Some key areas include personalization, targeted market segmentation, education, and brand recall and awareness.

An email list allows businesses to deliver personalized and targeted messaging to potential buyers, catering to their specific needs and interests. By segmenting the email list based on factors like demographics, preferences, or past interactions, businesses can create tailored email campaigns that resonate with each segment.

Nurturing potential buyers through an email list involves providing them with valuable information and educating them about the benefits and features of the products or services offered. By sharing useful content, you can address common pain points, provide solutions, and highlight the unique value proposition of their offerings.

Email newsletters, product guides, tutorials, or case studies can be powerful tools for educating potential buyers. These resources help customers understand how the product or service can meet their needs and solve their problems. By presenting valuable information in a clear and concise manner, businesses can position themselves as reliable sources of knowledge and build credibility among their audience.

An email list plays a vital role in building brand recall and awareness among potential buyers. By regularly appearing in their inboxes, businesses can keep their brand top-of-mind, even when customers are not actively considering a purchase. When the need arises, potential buyers are more likely to think of the brand they have been consistently engaging with, increasing the chances of conversion.

Additional Benefits of Email Lists

Email lists also provide small businesses with a significant return on investment and can even be automated to an extent.

For small businesses with limited marketing budgets, email marketing is a cost-effective solution that can deliver significant returns. Compared to traditional marketing channels like print media or direct mail, email campaigns require lower investments while offering a higher return on investment. Small businesses can promote their products or services directly to potential customers without the need for expensive advertising or distribution channels.

Additionally, email marketing platforms provide automation features that save time and resources. Small businesses can set up automated email sequences or trigger campaigns based on customer actions or specific events. This automation ensures consistent and timely communication with subscribers, even for businesses with limited manpower. It allows small businesses to focus on other critical aspects while maintaining a consistent presence in their customers' inboxes.

Small businesses thrive on building strong relationships with their customers, and an email list plays a crucial role in achieving this.

The important point is that if you grow your list, you are building your own pond to fish in. Not everyone is ready to buy right now, so your email list is a way to nurture people for the right time. It puts you in a prime position as the solution to their problems.

How to Build Your Email List

Building an email list is a lot easier than you might think. When it comes to building email lists, I want to stress three important points.

First off, building an email list is a long-term strategy. This means you have to commit to building it for the long haul. I've built a list of more than 260,000 people and it increases weekly. This list has been growing for years and has reached the point where the list brings me almost 90% of my revenue.

The second thing to stress is that you cannot let your email list go dormant; you need to be providing value to your list weekly. Think about it like a Netflix subscription: if people don't feel like they're getting value from it, they will unsubscribe. But if they're getting value, they will want to stay on the list. If you don't care for your list, it will go stale, and even the biggest of lists will stop producing revenue.

I run my list like clockwork. My email schedule consists of three emails each week. Monday's is value—something for the audience, Wednesday's is something for me—a call to action, and Friday's is a mix of promotion and value.

You might start with two emails per week, but it's important you deliver some value to your list and make clear offers to your subscribers. There's no point building a list if you aren't going to make money from it.

Finally, my third point: you want to build your list around your audience's dream outcome and pain point. If you build a list that is

139

too broad and unfocused, you'll struggle to keep people engaged. An unengaged list will eventually harm the deliverability of your emails and sender reputation.

The key is to grow a list of people who need what you sell. So building a list wrapped around your topic, pain points, and outcomes you deliver will avoid getting you into trouble with sending deliverability.

Let's look at some helpful and powerful techniques for building your email list.

1. Including a Sign-Up Form on Your Website

Adding a sign-up form for your email list on your website is a fundamental strategy to increase your subscriber base. This method involves creating a designated space on your website where visitors can willingly share their email addresses to become part of your email list. This approach is both straightforward and effective, and it can significantly contribute to the growth of your email list.

A sign-up form is essentially a digital tool that enables visitors to your website to provide their email addresses, demonstrating their interest in your content. You can strategically place this form on various pages of your website, such as the homepage, about page, individual blog posts, or even as a pop-up that appears when visitors are about to leave the site.

When creating your sign-up form, ensure that the design complements your website's overall look and feel. Simplicity and readability are key factors to consider. Keep the form concise by requesting only essential information like the visitor's name and email address. To entice visitors to subscribe, make sure you clearly communicate the benefits they will gain from signing up. A crucial element of your sign-up form is the call to action (CTA) button. Craft a compelling CTA that provides clear instructions, such as "Join Now" or

"Get Started." This button should prompt visitors to take action and become a part of your email list.

One of the major advantages of placing a sign-up form on your website is that it ensures the ability to join your email list is visible to your existing audience. Since visitors to your website are already interested in your content, the sign-up form provides an unobtrusive way for them to subscribe without leaving the site. This leads to a higher likelihood of capturing subscribers who are genuinely interested in what you have to offer.

Moreover, having control over the design, placement, and information collected from the sign-up form allows you to tailor the experience to align with your brand and your specific target audience. By gathering email addresses directly from your website, you obtain data from individuals who have shown a clear interest in your content. This targeted data can lead to better engagement rates when you send out your emails.

Your sign-up form on your website operates 24/7, providing a consistent means of capturing new subscribers. Even when you're not actively promoting your email list, the form remains available and continues to attract potential subscribers who stumble upon your website.

2. Pinning to Your Profiles on Social Media

Another effective way to grow your email list is by utilizing a pinned link on your social media profiles. On Instagram, X, Facebook, and TikTok, you can add links into your bio—use them!

This strategy involves strategically placing a prominent link at the top of your social media profiles, making it easily accessible to anyone who visits your profile. This method takes advantage of your existing social media following and directs them to join your email list for more exclusive content and updates.

A pinned link is essentially a link that you can attach to the top of your social media profiles, ensuring it's one of the first things visitors see when they land on your page. This link serves as an invitation for your social media audience to subscribe to your email list and stay connected with your content on a deeper level.

Why is this strategy effective? Well, your social media followers are already interested in your content and brand, which means they're more likely to engage with your email communications as well. By placing a pinned link on your profile, you're capitalizing on this existing interest and encouraging your social media audience to take the next step in their engagement with your brand.

When creating the pinned link, ensure that the destination page is relevant and appealing to your target audience. Clearly communicate the benefits of subscribing to your email list, such as receiving exclusive updates, behind-the-scenes insights, or valuable resources that they won't find anywhere else.

It's worth noting that some social media platforms often allow you to include a short description along with your pinned link. Use this space wisely to provide a brief explanation of what visitors can expect when they click the link and join your email list. A well-crafted description can help entice more of your social media followers to take action.

Final tip: make sure the sign-up page of your link is mobile friendly. The last thing you want is people not signing up because it was too difficult on their mobile phone.

3. Creating a Lead Magnet and Landing Page

A lead magnet is a powerful tool in the world of online marketing, designed to attract and engage potential customers. Essentially, it's a valuable piece of content that you offer to your audience in exchange for their contact information, most commonly their email addresses. The idea is simple yet effective: you provide something enticing enough that people willingly share their details with you.

Think of a lead magnet as a "gift" to your audience. It could take various forms, such as an e-book, a downloadable guide, a webinar, a video tutorial, a checklist, a template, a discount code, or any other resource that addresses a specific problem or fulfills a particular need your target audience has.

The key to a successful lead magnet lies in its relevance and value. It should provide instant gratification by offering immediate solutions, insights, or benefits to the recipient. For instance, if you're running a fitness blog, your lead magnet could be a downloadable workout plan tailored to beginners. If you're a business consultant, a lead magnet might be a guide on improving productivity.

By offering a lead magnet, you're not only providing value up front, but you're also starting a relationship with your audience. Once someone has received your lead magnet, they're more likely to engage further with your content and offerings. This helps you nurture leads and guide them along the customer journey.

To effectively harness the potential of a lead magnet, you'll want to promote it strategically. Place it prominently on your website, within blog posts, and even on your social media profiles. Create compelling calls to action that emphasize the benefits of your lead magnet, encouraging visitors to take action.

In the end, a lead magnet serves as the entry point to your sales funnel. It piques the interest of potential customers, demonstrates your expertise, and initiates a connection that can evolve into a long-lasting customer relationship. By offering something of value in exchange for contact information, you're not just growing your email list—you're setting the stage for meaningful engagement and mutual benefit.

When constructing a lead magnet landing page, several key elements need to be considered. The headline, for instance, should succinctly convey the value of your lead magnet and outline the benefits for visitors. Engaging copy is essential; it should clearly explain how the lead magnet addresses a particular problem and enhances the lives of those who access it.

Visual elements such as high-quality images or graphics should be incorporated, connecting with the content of the lead magnet and resonating with your target audience. The inclusion of an opt-in form allows visitors to provide their email addresses in exchange for the lead magnet. Simplicity is key here; ask for only essential information to avoid overwhelming potential subscribers.

A strong call-to-action (CTA) button is crucial in guiding visitors toward the next step. The language used should be action-oriented and instructive, such as "Download Now" or "Get Your Free Guide." Social proof, like testimonials or endorsements, can also bolster your credibility and assure visitors of the lead magnet's value.

To build trust and privacy, clearly communicate that the email addresses collected will be kept confidential and not shared with third parties. After submitting their email addresses, visitors should be redirected to a thank-you page where they can access the lead magnet and receive further instructions.

Ultimately, this strategy is effective because it not only encourages visitors to become subscribers but also offers them tangible value from the very beginning of their engagement with your brand. By presenting something beneficial and relevant, you're more likely to gain email addresses from individuals who are genuinely interested in your content. This, in turn, creates a solid foundation for ongoing engagement and interaction with your audience through your email communications.

4. Conducting Educational Webinars

I love doing educational webinars. I run one live each week and get sign-ups organically from social media. The great part about it is that while I'm building my email list, I'm also demonstrating my expertise.

One of the core advantages of webinars lies in their ability to deliver engaging content. By diving deep into a specific topic, you offer in-depth insights, practical tips, and problem-solving techniques. This showcase of your expertise positions you as a credible and trusted authority within your industry or niche.

To attract an audience and capture their attention, strategically promote your upcoming webinar across various channels. Craft compelling headlines that highlight the value participants will gain from attending. As individuals register for the webinar, you collect their email addresses, thereby organically increasing your contact list.

I like to build my sign-up forms on platforms like Eventbrite. The beauty is that I have a list I can share across all social media platforms. You can build a sign-up page on your website, but I've found it simpler and easier to use Eventbrite; it's trusted and has millions of users, so you can pick up registrations just from posting on their platform.

I don't use ads; I just promote the webinars across social media. I'll post about them, message some of my followers and connections, and my team will do the same.

During the webinar itself, encourage active participation through features like Q&A sessions, polls, and discussions. This interactive approach not only enhances the learning experience but also fosters a sense of connection between you and your audience.

Following the conclusion of the webinar, maintain the connection by sending a thoughtful follow-up email. Express gratitude for attendees' participation and provide access to the webinar recording or any additional resources promised. This post-webinar communication continues the engagement and sustains their interest.

Webinar attendees who find value in your content are more likely to engage with your subsequent emails and offerings. By consistently delivering relevant and valuable content, you can nurture these leads over time, gradually guiding them through the customer journey.

5. Commenting for Access

This technique is one of my absolute favorites when it comes to beefing up my email list. And the kicker? It's not just about the numbers; this will give a serious boost to my social media content too.

You've got a neat little template or a nifty method that can help people hit a particular goal. It could be anything, such as a template on how to write social media posts, or a quick way to achieve a task. Instead of posting a link, I play it a bit cooler. I put out a post giving a teaser of the value and I ask the people who want it to comment with a word or phrase. I'll tell people in my post, "Leave the comment 'PDF' and I'll send you a copy."

Now here's where the magic happens. Those curious people who wanna grab that solution for themselves leave a comment and amplify the post. After four or five comments you'll find your post is reaching more and more people. This is a smart way to create a win-win. It yields higher engagement, which brings you more leads.

What do you do next? Well, you drop a direct message (DM) with the sign-up link to everyone who commented. Once you've sent the link you reply to the comments and let them know you've sent them a message with the details.

This method is not just about building your list, but increasing your visibility online too.

6. Running a Permission-Based DM Campaign

Sending spammy direct messages (DMs) to sell services is something nobody wants to do. However, there's an effective approach to build your email list using DMs. This process involves offering valuable content through a permission-based DM campaign to your ideal clients, ultimately helping you connect, engage, and grow your email list.

To start, you need to create a valuable asset, such as a guide or template, that provides quick and tangible benefits to your audience. This content should address a specific problem or help your audience achieve a small goal. This content becomes the centerpiece of your campaign.

Identify individuals within your social media network, followers, connections, and even Facebook friends, who align with your ideal client profile. These are the people who would benefit the most from your valuable content. You'll send them a personalized message, offering to share the guide or template you've created. You seek their permission to send them the content. After they've agreed, you request their email address to deliver the content effectively.

With their email addresses secured, you promptly send them the promised content. As an added touch, you can let them know that you'll continue sending them valuable insights related to the same topic or outcome via email.

This strategy opens the door to meaningful conversations and follow-up opportunities. You can ask recipients how they found the content, if it was helpful, and initiate genuine conversations that can lead to stronger connections.

Engaging in conversations about the content you shared can create a pathway to showcasing your expertise and potentially converting recipients into clients.

While the process is generally straightforward, there are a few points to keep in mind about automation. Although automation might seem like a time-saver, social media platforms often frown upon excessive use of automation. Overusing automation could result in platform restrictions. It's essential to stay within the guidelines of each platform to ensure your account remains in good standing. Avoid using automated messages to maintain a genuine and human touch.

In a world where spammy marketing approaches are often ignored, permission-based DM campaigns offer a refreshing and effective way to grow your email list and foster genuine connections.

The Bottom Line

Growing your email list is a daily activity; each day one of your social media channels could be growing your list. Make sure you make the most of this long-term strategy to make your business algorithm.

Without my email list, I would have struggled during the pandemic. In 2020, I went into lockdown with more than a hundred thousand people signed up. That enabled my business to keep going when everything was shuttered.

The biggest mistake is putting "getting a client" in front of "getting clients." Because building an email list requires a "little and often" approach, it's easy to neglect, but almost nobody ever regrets building an email list.

Chapter 10

Creating Compelling Copy That Converts Prospects into Paying Clients

Copywriting is a crucial skill in today's business world. It doesn't require a formal education or expert-level skills, but it is essential for crafting landing pages, blogs, social media posts, and persuasive emails. With the countless tips and advice available online, mastering copywriting can feel overwhelming, especially for those new to the process. That's why it's important to have practical and straightforward tips that will help you master copywriting effectively.

Regardless of whatever you're writing, being authentic is key. There's nothing worse than trying to write in a style that doesn't feel natural. Your primary objective is to get people to know, like, and trust you, and that's best achieved by showcasing your unique voice.

In the past, formal or journalistic styles were the norm, but that has changed. Today, readers appreciate a more conversational style. Of course, there are some general rules about spelling, grammar, and punctuation, but today's society allows for a bit more flexibility, particularly with social media posts and blogs. Your copy should be easy to follow and engaging for online consumption, where attention spans are shorter.

When crafting your copy, it's important to strike a balance between addressing your audience's pain points and highlighting the positive outcomes they can achieve. People are motivated to take action when they're dissatisfied with their current situation. By tapping into that dissatisfaction and offering a solution, you can drive action.

While it's essential to weave in pain points to show that there is a cost to staying in their current situation, your copy should focus on outcomes, goals, and aspirations, as that's where people want to go. Your copy should be optimistic, goal-centric, and outcome-centric, but also highlight the problems or pains of not taking action.

Engaging the Emotions

The purpose of great copywriting is to persuade people, and that means touching their emotions. You should aim to create a picture in your readers' minds and connect with them on an emotional level. People are more inclined to remember and be influenced by words that evoke emotions.

Experiment with language to create drama and emotion in your writing, even for B2B. Use questions to make your readers feel something. Remember, emotions drive decisions. People decide with emotion and justify with logic. By creating an emotional connection with your audience, you make your copy more impactful and persuasive.

Effective copywriting is about being authentic, balancing pain and gain, using proven frameworks, and engaging emotions. By following these principles, you can create copy that resonates with your audience and drives them to take action.

Structuring Your Writing

One of the biggest challenges in copywriting is knowing where to start and what structure to follow. There are many proven copywriting formulas to help you put together effective copy. These frameworks offer a flow and structure for your copy, making it more persuasive.

Several popular and practical frameworks and techniques exist and are fairly easy to learn:

- AIDA (Attention, Interest, Desire, Action)
- PAS (Problem, Agitate, Solution)
- FAB (Features, Advantages, Benefits)
- The Four Cs (Clear, Concise, Compelling, Credible)
- The Four Ps (Promise, Picture, Proof, Push)
- The Bridge Method

These methods provide a structure for crafting copy that appeals to your audience's emotions, painting a picture in their mind. Which structure should you use? Whichever you like. Professional copywriters normally have a favored method that is their go-to. You can use one or all of them. I tend to use the PAS framework most of the time, but also like the Bridge Method. You'll learn about the different methods next.

AIDA (Attention, Interest, Desire, Action)

One of the most well-known and effective copywriting frameworks, AIDA is a simple, four-step formula that helps you create persuasive copy that captures your audience's attention, stokes their interest and desire, and ultimately prompts them to take action. Let's dive into each step and learn how to apply it with practical tips.

Attention: Drawing Your Reader's Notice

The first step is to get your reader's attention. With so much content vying for our attention, you need a strong hook to stand out. The best way to capture attention is with a compelling headline or opening statement:

- Craft a headline that is intriguing, promises a benefit, or poses a question.

- Use numbers, questions, or power words to create a sense of urgency or curiosity.

- Be specific and relevant to your target audience's needs or pain points.

Instead of writing "Learn to manage your finances," try something more attention-grabbing, like "Discover the five secrets to achieving financial freedom and living the life you've always dreamed of."

Interest: Building Curiosity and Engagement

Once you've grabbed your reader's attention, you need to hold it by creating interest. This is where you explore the problem or need your audience is facing, offer insights or new perspectives, and hint at a solution:

- Present a problem or question that resonates with your audience.

- Share a surprising fact, statistic, or anecdote related to the problem.

- Tease the benefits or results of your solution without giving away all the details.

Continuing the financial freedom example, you could write, "Did you know that 65% of Americans struggle to save money, even though they earn decent salaries? The problem isn't your income—it's how you manage it. Imagine being able to take that dream vacation, buy a new car, or retire comfortably, all without stressing about money."

Desire: Creating an Emotional Connection

The next step is to create desire for your product or service by show-casing its benefits. Appeal to your audience's emotions by describing how your solution will improve their lives, alleviate their pain points, or help them achieve their goals:

- Focus on the benefits, not just the features, of your product or service.

- Use emotive language that taps into your audience's aspirations or frustrations.

- Show the transformation your solution offers, either through before-and-after examples, testimonials, or compelling imagery.

For example, "With our financial coaching program, you'll finally break free from the paycheck-to-paycheck cycle and start enjoying life on your terms. Our clients have paid off thousands in debt, saved for their dream homes, and even retired early. You deserve to live a life free from financial stress, and we're here to help you achieve it."

Action: Prompting Your Reader to Take the Next Step

The final step in the AIDA framework is to prompt your reader to take action. Whether you want them to sign up for a newsletter, make a purchase, or schedule a consultation, your call to action should be clear, compelling, and easy to follow:

- Use strong, action-oriented verbs in your CTA (e.g., "Get started," "Learn more," "Join now").

- Create a sense of urgency or scarcity to encourage immediate action (e.g., "Limited-time offer," "Only a few spots left").

- Make it easy for your reader to take action by providing a clear and accessible next step, such as a prominent button or link.

For example, "Ready to take control of your financial future? Join our financial coaching program today and start experiencing the freedom you deserve. But don't wait—spaces are limited, and this offer ends soon. Click the link below to get started now."

When writing your copy, remember that the AIDA framework is a flexible guide. You can adjust the length and depth of each section based on your specific needs and audience. The key is to create a flow that captures attention, engages interest, stokes desire, and prompts action. By applying these practical tips and examples, you'll be on your way to crafting compelling copy that resonates with your audience and drives results.

PAS (Problem, Agitate, Solution)

The PAS framework is a simple yet powerful copywriting technique that can create compelling and persuasive copy. It taps into human emotions, focusing on a specific problem faced by your target audience, intensifying the emotions surrounding the problem, and then presenting a solution.

Identify the Problem

The first step in the PAS framework is to pinpoint a problem that your target audience is experiencing. By addressing a specific problem that resonates with your audience, you immediately capture their attention and demonstrate that you understand their needs.

To identify the most relevant problem, conduct market research, analyze customer feedback, and empathize with your audience. Once you have identified the problem, open your copy by clearly stating it. Use simple language that speaks directly to the reader, showing that you understand their pain points.

For example, "Are you tired of wasting hours trying to find a parking space every day?"

Agitate the Problem

After identifying the problem, the next step is to agitate or intensify the emotions associated with the problem. This stage is essential because it connects with the reader on an emotional level, making them more inclined to take action. By describing the negative consequences, frustrations, and impact of the problem on the reader's life, you help them see the urgency of finding a solution.

Use descriptive language to paint a vivid picture of the problem's implications. Describe how the problem affects the reader's daily life, relationships, work, and overall well-being. Make sure your language is relatable and resonates with the reader's emotions.

For example, "The search for a parking space can be incredibly frustrating. You circle the block multiple times, getting more irritated with each passing minute. Your morning coffee gets cold, your workday starts late, and you feel stressed even before your day has truly begun."

Present the Solution

After agitating the problem, it's time to present your product or service as the solution to the reader's pain points. This is your opportunity to showcase the value your product or service provides and explain how it addresses the specific problem you identified.

Clearly explain the features and benefits of your product or service. Use language that emphasizes how your solution alleviates the problem and improves the reader's situation. Be specific about what your product or service offers and how it addresses the pain points you've discussed.

For example, "With our parking app, you can easily find and reserve a parking space before you even leave your home. No more driving in circles, no more stress, and no more wasted time. Simply open the app, choose a spot, and park your car with ease."

Call to Action

After presenting the solution, conclude your copy with a strong and clear call to action (CTA) that prompts the reader to take the next step. Whether you want them to sign up, make a purchase, or learn more, your CTA should be compelling and actionable.

Make your CTA specific and actionable. Use persuasive language that encourages the reader to take the next step immediately. Make it easy for the reader to act by providing a clear path to the desired action.

For example, "Download our app today and say goodbye to parking stress! Reserve your spot now and enjoy a hassle-free start to your day."

Additional Tips for PAS Copywriting

You can use these techniques to take your PAS copy to the next level:

- Put yourself in the shoes of your target audience. Understand their needs, emotions, and pain points. The more you can relate to their experiences, the more effective your copy will be.

- Use language that resonates with your audience. Choose words that evoke emotions, paint vivid pictures, and are easily relatable.

- Keep your copy concise and focused. Stay on topic, avoid unnecessary jargon, and get to the point quickly.

- Provide evidence that supports your claims. Share testimonials, reviews, or case studies that showcase how your product or service has successfully solved similar problems for others.

- Highlight the unique value proposition of your product or service. What sets you apart from the competition? Why should the reader choose your solution over others?

- Anticipate potential objections or concerns your audience may have and address them within your copy. Reassure the reader that your solution is the right choice.

The PAS copywriting framework is a powerful tool for creating persuasive copy that connects with the reader on an emotional level. By identifying a specific problem, agitating it, and presenting a solution, you can create copy that resonates with your audience and prompts them to take action.

FAB (Features, Advantages, Benefits)

The FAB framework is a popular copywriting tool used to create persuasive and compelling copy that resonates with the reader and compels them to take action. In essence, by highlighting the Features, Advantages, and Benefits, the FAB framework helps readers understand how a product or service can address their needs and improve their lives.

Features

Start by listing the features of your product or service. Features are the tangible aspects of your product or service—the things that make it unique or special. Features can include attributes such as size, color, specifications, capabilities, components, or any other details that describe your product or service:

- Make a comprehensive list of all the features of your product or service.

- Use clear and specific language to describe each feature.

- If applicable, provide technical specifications to cater to a more informed audience.

Consider a smartphone as the product. Features could include a 6.5-inch OLED display, 5G connectivity, a 108 MP camera, a water-resistant design, and a 4500mAh battery.

Advantages

Next, discuss the advantages of each feature. Advantages are the reasons why each feature is beneficial or valuable compared to other options on the market. Advantages explain how the features of your product or service stand out from the competition:

- Highlight the uniqueness of each feature.
- Consider the alternatives that your audience might be considering and explain why your product or service has an edge.
- Be specific about how each feature provides value or offers a superior experience.

For the smartphone example, the advantages could include an ultra-clear and vibrant display for an immersive viewing experience, faster and more reliable internet connectivity, a high-resolution camera for professional-quality photos, enhanced durability for peace of mind, and a long-lasting battery for all-day usage.

Benefits

Finally, articulate the benefits of your product or service. Benefits are the positive outcomes or improvements that the reader can expect to experience by using your product or service. Benefits are often emotional and focus on how the reader's life will be better, easier, or more enjoyable:

- Focus on the end user's perspective.
- Address the reader's pain points and explain how your product or service can alleviate them.

- Use emotional language to connect with the reader and evoke a response.

For the smartphone example, the benefits could include enjoying an enhanced entertainment experience with a stunning display, staying connected with friends and family without interruptions, capturing cherished memories in stunning detail, having peace of mind when using the phone in wet conditions, and not having to worry about the battery running out in the middle of the day.

The FAB framework is a versatile and powerful tool for crafting persuasive and compelling copy. By systematically presenting the features, advantages, and benefits of your product or service, you can effectively address the needs and desires of your target audience, connect with them on an emotional level, and persuade them to take action. As a copywriter, be sure to employ this framework as you create copy for various channels such as websites, advertisements, product descriptions, and more. The FAB framework is a proven method for generating interest, building trust, and driving conversions.

Remember, the key is to create a narrative that resonates with the reader and compels them to take action. Be genuine, specific, and relatable in your messaging, and always prioritize the reader's needs and desires. With the right approach, the FAB framework can be a highly effective tool for creating compelling copy that converts.

The Four Cs (Clear, Concise, Compelling, Credible)

The Four Cs copywriting framework is a simple yet effective approach to writing persuasive copy that resonates with your audience and drives them to take action. By following the principles of being Clear, Concise, Compelling, and Credible, you can craft powerful

Copy That Converts Prospects into Paying Clients

copy that converts. Here we delve deeper into each of the Four Cs and provide practical tips to apply them in your copywriting.

Clear

Clear copy is easily understood by the reader. It's important to use simple language and avoid jargon, technical terms, or complex sentence structures. Your message should be straightforward, and your reader should know exactly what you're offering and what action you want them to take:

- **Know Your Audience:** Understand the language and terminology that resonates with your target audience. Use their words and phrases to connect with them more effectively.
- **Simplify Your Sentences:** Use short sentences and avoid complex sentence structures. Break up long paragraphs into shorter, more digestible ones.
- **Avoid Jargon:** Unless your audience is highly specialized, avoid industry-specific jargon or technical terms. If you must use them, provide clear explanations.

Concise

Concise copy is brief and to the point. In the age of short attention spans, readers appreciate copy that gets straight to the point without any unnecessary fluff. Every word should serve a purpose and contribute to the overall message.

- **Eliminate Redundancy:** Remove redundant words or phrases that don't add value to your message. For example, instead of "free gift," just say "gift."

- **Be Specific:** Replace vague words with specific, descriptive terms. For example, instead of "a lot," say "hundreds" or "thousands."

- **Use Strong Verbs:** Choose action-oriented verbs that convey a sense of movement or progress. For example, instead of "make an improvement," say "enhance."

Compelling

Compelling copy grabs the reader's attention and evokes an emotional response. It's persuasive and engaging, and it encourages the reader to take action, whether that's making a purchase, signing up for a newsletter, or sharing content on social media:

- **Tell a Story:** People love stories, and they can be a powerful way to connect with your audience. Share a customer success story or describe a scenario where your product or service made a difference.

- **Use Emotional Triggers:** Identify the emotions that drive your audience to take action, whether it's excitement, curiosity, or even fear of missing out. Craft your copy to evoke these emotions.

- **Create a Sense of Urgency:** Use phrases like "limited time offer," "only a few left," or "sale ends soon" to create a sense of urgency and encourage immediate action.

Credible

Credible copy is trustworthy and believable. Readers are more likely to take action if they believe the claims you make in your copy. Supporting your claims with evidence, such as testimonials, statistics, or expert endorsements, can enhance your credibility.

Copy That Converts Prospects into Paying Clients

- **Provide Social Proof:** Share testimonials, reviews, or case studies from satisfied customers. If possible, include the customer's name, title, and company for added credibility.

- **Use Statistics:** Provide data or statistics that support your claims. Ensure that your sources are reputable and that you present the information accurately.

- **Show Credentials:** If you or your company have relevant credentials or endorsements from industry experts, include them in your copy. This can help establish your authority and expertise in your field.

The Four Cs copywriting framework provides a practical and effective approach to crafting persuasive copy that resonates with your audience. By being Clear, Concise, Compelling, and Credible, you can create copy that captures attention, builds trust, and drives action. Keep these principles in mind as you craft your copy.

The Four Ps (Promise, Picture, Proof, Push)

In the world of copywriting, one of the most effective and commonly used frameworks is the Four Ps model. This model incorporates four key components: Promise, Picture, Proof, and Push. When combined, these four elements can create a persuasive piece of copy that engages readers and compels them to take action. Here's a closer look at the Four Ps, along with some practical tips to help you apply them effectively.

Promise

First, you make a clear and enticing promise to your readers that addresses a specific need or desire they have. This promise should be bold and intriguing, capturing your audience's attention and making them want to learn more:

- **Identify Your Audience's Pain Points:** Understand your target audience and their pain points. What problems or challenges are they facing? What do they desire?

- **Make a Bold Claim:** Your promise should be strong enough to grab the reader's attention. Make a claim that resonates with their needs and desires.

- **Be Specific:** Be specific in your promise. Avoid vague or generic statements. Clearly articulate what you're offering and how it will benefit the reader.

For example, "Discover how to increase your website traffic by 200% in just 30 days!"

Picture

Next, you paint a vivid picture in the reader's mind of what life will be like once they've taken advantage of your offer. By evoking strong emotions and appealing to their imagination, you make your copy more compelling and relatable.

- **Use Descriptive Language:** Use language that appeals to the senses. Make the reader "see" and "feel" the benefits of your offer.

- **Tell a Story:** Storytelling is a powerful tool. Share a relatable story or anecdote that illustrates the transformation your product or service can provide.

- **Highlight Emotional Benefits:** Go beyond tangible benefits. Highlight the emotional benefits your reader will experience, such as peace of mind, happiness, or satisfaction.

For example, "Imagine a world where your website is bustling with activity, leads are pouring in, and sales are skyrocketing. You can finally relax, knowing that your business is thriving."

Proof

At this stage, you provide evidence—proof—that supports your claims. This can include testimonials, case studies, expert endorsements, or any other form of proof that establishes credibility and builds trust with your readers:

- **Show Real Results:** Share real-life results that customers have achieved using your product or service. This could be in the form of before-and-after photos, testimonials, or case studies.

- **Use Statistics:** Share relevant statistics or data that support your claims. This adds credibility to your copy.

- **Leverage Authority Figures:** If you have endorsements or testimonials from industry experts, influencers, or well-known figures, use them to your advantage. This enhances your credibility.

For example, "Our program has helped over 1,000 businesses double their website traffic. But don't just take our word for it. Listen to what industry expert John Smith has to say: 'This program is a game-changer. I've seen remarkable results in just a few weeks.'"

Push

Finally, the push is where you provide a strong and compelling call to action that encourages the reader to take the desired action. Your CTA should be clear, concise, and direct:

- **Make It Urgent:** Create a sense of urgency by adding a time-sensitive offer or highlighting a limited quantity.

- **Be Direct:** Clearly state what action you want the reader to take. Use action words such as "sign up," "buy," or "download."

- **Provide Incentives:** Offer something valuable in exchange for taking action, such as a discount, freebie, or bonus.

For example, "Don't miss out on this opportunity to skyrocket your website traffic. Sign up for our program today and receive a 20% discount. This offer expires in 48 hours, so act now!"

The Bridge Method

In the world of copywriting, the Bridge Method is a popular technique used to persuade readers to take a particular action, whether it's purchasing a product, signing up for a newsletter, or scheduling an appointment. The central idea behind this method is to connect the reader's current situation (the "before" state) with a desired future situation (the "after" state) by introducing your product or service as the bridge that will get them there.

Let's take a look at a step-by-step breakdown of how to use the Bridge Method, along with practical tips for each stage.

Identify and Acknowledge the Current Situation

Start by recognizing the reader's current situation, including any problems or pain points they're experiencing. This step involves understanding your target audience's needs and presenting them in a way that resonates.

Use empathy to put yourself in the reader's shoes. Use language that reflects their emotions and experiences. If you're marketing a fitness program, for example, you could start with, "Are you tired of feeling sluggish and out of shape, struggling to find the motivation to work out?"

Present the Bridge

Introduce your product or service as the "bridge" that can take them from their current situation to the desired one. Clearly explain how your offering will address their pain points and make their lives better.

Use language that emphasizes transformation and progress. Continuing with the fitness program example, you could say, "Our 30-day fitness challenge is designed to help you jump-start your fitness journey and transform your life."

Paint a Picture of the Future Situation

Describe the positive outcome or benefits the reader will experience by using your product or service. Create a compelling and vivid picture of what life will be like once they've crossed the bridge.

Use descriptive language that appeals to the senses and emotions. In the fitness program example, you could say, "Imagine waking up feeling energized and refreshed, ready to take on the day with newfound confidence and vitality."

End with a Compelling Call to Action

Close your copy with a strong call to action that encourages the reader to take the desired action and cross the bridge.

Make your CTA specific, clear, and urgent. For the fitness program, you could say, "Join our 30-day fitness challenge now and start your transformation today!"

Additional Tips for Using the Bridge Method

You can use these techniques to make using the Bridge Method even more powerful:

- **Use Stories:** Incorporate stories or testimonials from people who have successfully crossed the bridge with your product or service. This adds credibility to your claims and shows readers that the transformation is possible.

- **Address Objections:** Anticipate any objections or barriers that might prevent your readers from taking action. Address these objections in your copy to reassure readers and make it easier for them to cross the bridge.

- **Highlight Unique Selling Propositions (USPs):** Identify what makes your product or service unique and highlight these USPs in your copy. This helps your offering stand out from the competition and shows readers why your bridge is the best option.

- **Create a Sense of Urgency:** Encourage readers to take action sooner rather than later by creating a sense of urgency. You could use limited-time offers, exclusive bonuses, or scarcity tactics to motivate readers to cross the bridge now.

- **Keep It Relatable:** Make sure your bridge is relatable to your target audience. If you're selling a high-end product, for example, you wouldn't want to target individuals who can't afford it. Similarly, if your product requires a certain level of skill or knowledge, make sure you're targeting the right audience.

- **Test and Tweak:** The effectiveness of your copy will depend on various factors, including your target audience, the product or service you're offering, and the specific pain points you're addressing. It's important to test different approaches, analyze the results, and tweak your copy accordingly to optimize its performance.

Remember to use empathy, vivid language, and stories to create a strong emotional connection with your readers. And don't forget to address objections, highlight USPs, create urgency, keep it relatable, and test and tweak for optimal results.

You didn't start a business to become a copywriter, but it's important to do the best job you can to create copy that is persuasive. Learning some of the key copywriting methods will help you bring structure to your writing and will help you write the most persuasive sales and marketing copy to help you convert more leads and inquiries.

Chapter 11

Handling Inquiries and Discovery Calls

With all the practical information in this book, you will be very busy generating leads and inquiries but now comes the most important bit: turning that interest into paying clients and customers.

How you handle an inquiry will determine your "close rate," which is essentially your success rate at turning interest into sales. This isn't so much about being the best salesperson, but it is about understanding how people buy and transact.

Speed is an essential factor in following up with leads and inquiries, playing a crucial role in successfully converting prospects into potential customers. When a prospect shows interest in your product or service, their enthusiasm is at its peak. Responding quickly to their inquiries allows you to capitalize on this enthusiasm and increases the likelihood of conversion.

Being quick to follow up also gives you a competitive advantage. In a crowded market, prospects often consider multiple options, and the first company to respond can leave a lasting impression. By being the first to follow up, you have the chance to engage with the prospect before your competitors and establish a strong connection.

Quick follow-up also increases the chances of converting leads into customers. Prospects often have questions or concerns that need to be addressed before making a purchasing decision. By responding promptly, you can provide the necessary information, address any objections, and build trust. This timely interaction makes it more likely that the prospect will choose your offering over others.

Finally, speed in follow-up helps maintain momentum in the sales process. When a lead expresses interest, there is an inherent level of excitement and engagement. Quickly following up allows you to capitalize on this momentum and keep the conversation moving forward, increasing the chances of moving the lead through the sales funnel and closing the deal.

Do You Need a Call?

If you are selling high-value services, you will likely need to have a conversation with a prospect. While you can respond to inquiries by email and give quotes and proposals without ever speaking to a client, it can be dangerous.

Have you ever played the telephone game? A group of friends whispers to each other a word or phrase, passing it around the group one person at a time. As the whisper goes around, each person interprets it differently. Simple phrases can quickly get lost and jumbled. When I played it at school as a child, one time we started with "She sells seashells by the seashore." By the time it was whispered around a small group, it had become "Sheila sells ice cream on the bathroom floor."

So remember, things can get lost in translation. Although you can go back and forth with a prospect by email, it's easy for the prospect to miss the value of your offer or proposal. That's why a discovery call is always preferred to help clarify what a prospect needs and help you propose the best option for them.

The other big reason to offer a discovery call is that if the prospect is looking to make a large purchase, you will want to build some rapport with them, so keeping things to email could work against you.

What Is a Discovery Call?

A discovery call is an initial conversation between you and a prospective client or lead. This type of call is typically the first step in the sales process and serves as a foundation for building a relationship with the prospective client.

Discovery calls are an essential component of the consultative selling approach, where a seller acts more like a trusted advisor rather than a traditional salesperson. In this approach, the goal is to understand the prospect's specific needs and offer tailored solutions that can help them achieve their goals. If you don't want to transform into a salesperson, the best way to sell is through a consultative approach.

During a discovery call, your aim is to gather as much information as possible about the prospect's current situation, goals, and challenges. This information is then used to tailor the sales pitch, demonstrate the value of the product or service, and create a compelling case for why the prospect should consider making a purchase.

The key aspects of a successful discovery call include asking open-ended questions, actively listening to the prospect's responses, and building rapport. It is important to note that discovery calls are not meant to be overly sales-focused. Instead, they should focus on understanding the prospect's needs and building a foundation for a productive and mutually beneficial relationship.

Once you've started the call and said your hello, there is a defined structure to most successful discovery calls. They generally follow this pattern:

1. **Preparing for the Call:** Doing a little research can go a long way in ensuring your call will be more successful.

2. **Breaking the Ice:** As you start the call with a prospect, you need to engage in small talk to build a connection with the prospect. This helps create a comfortable atmosphere for the conversation and can lead to more open and honest communication.

3. **Setting the Agenda:** Once you have broken the ice, you want to outline the meeting, what they are looking for, and how the call will flow.

4. **Discovery:** Don't think of this stage as an interrogation; it's more about understanding where the prospect is at right now and what they want to achieve. This is the most crucial part of the discovery call, because it provides valuable insights that will shape the rest of the sales process.

5. **Mirroring Back:** This part is simple; you simply confirm your understanding of what they are looking for and affirm their concerns, pain points, goals, and timescales.

6. **Presenting Your Offer:** This is where you transition to making your offer to them of how you could help. First off, you make some broad recommendations that fit into how you deliver your product or service. The key is to offer value.

7. **Scheduling Next Steps:** Now you need to agree on the next steps in the sales process, including sending a proposal, a follow-up meeting, product demonstration, or proposal presentation.

8. **Following Up:** Once you've finished the call, the next step is tactful, consistent follow-up to ensure everything goes smoothly.

We'll look at these stages in a bit more detail.

Preparing for the Call

Before you ever reach a discovery call you should do some research to check out the company and the prospect on LinkedIn. Look at how the company is doing, whether they have hired recently, and what their website shares about company updates.

Why is this important? Not only can research help you know who you're meeting, but it can help you understand the context of your conversation. For example, if your prospect is in a large business, do they have buying authority? How would this person leverage your products and services?

But we can go deeper. If the company is growing and hiring, this is a positive indication that the company is investing in growth. Doing research will help you prepare for the call, and as you discuss the prospects' needs, you can see why and how they could potentially work in their organization. Research is also helpful in preventing you from suggesting ideas that may not work in their organization; the aim of the call is to understand their needs and see how you can help solve them, but the prospect needs to be convinced that your offer is the right fit for them. In other words, can you solve the problem in a way that works for them? Research will help you make that discovery call go more smoothly and help your prospect see you are a potential good fit.

Breaking the Ice

Breaking the ice is an essential first step in any sales call. It helps set a positive tone, puts both parties at ease, and lays the groundwork for a more productive conversation. It's not always easy to achieve, but with a few simple strategies, you can quickly establish rapport and make your prospect feel comfortable. Here are some tips to help you break the ice and start your discovery call on the right foot.

Look for Common Ground

Before the call, do some research on your prospect. Check their LinkedIn profile, company website, or other online presence for any personal or professional information that you might have in common. Maybe you went to the same school, share a hobby, or have mutual connections. Mentioning these shared experiences can be a great way to start the conversation on a positive note and build rapport.

Comment on Their Space

In the age of video calls, it's common to get a glimpse of your prospect's workspace or home office. If you notice something interesting or unique in their background, feel free to comment on it. Whether it's a piece of art, a bookshelf, or even a cute pet, showing interest in their personal space can help establish a connection.

In my office, I have a large collection of model spaceships from *Star Trek*; this always becomes an ice breaker because they are prominent on calls. I often look for notable objects in the background of the call as a way to put everyone at ease.

Use the Weather

Talking about the weather might sound cliché, but it's a universal topic that can help break the ice. Especially if your prospect is located in a different region or country, asking about their local weather can be a natural way to start the conversation.

I'm British, so I love using the weather as a means to break the ice. When I'm talking to international clients, I often ask them about the weather where they are and complain about the British weather. It's a great tool for establishing rapport. I'm a fan of tropical climates, so when it's raining in the UK, I have a lot to say!

Keep It Light and Casual

When breaking the ice, aim for a casual and friendly tone. Avoid diving straight into business matters or getting too formal. A little small talk can go a long way in establishing a relaxed atmosphere. Ask how their day is going or if they have any plans for the weekend.

Use Humor

A light-hearted joke or comment can help ease any tension and set a positive tone for the conversation. Make sure your humor is appropriate for the situation and consider the prospect's cultural background to avoid any misunderstandings.

I'm rubbish at jokes, but one thing I've found is that you often will repeat the same things on different discovery calls. Having a few funny stories up your sleeve can help out when you get started. Just be careful not to push the envelope with humor, because not everyone's sense of humor is the same.

Compliment Their Achievements

If you've done your research and know about recent successes or milestones achieved by your prospect or their company, don't hesitate to offer a genuine compliment. It shows that you've done your homework and are interested in their success.

This only works if it's something worth complimenting. Nobody likes a "suck-up," as they say, so try to avoid complimenting unless it is something significant. For example, if they are new into a role, you can say you checked their LinkedIn beforehand and ask them how they are finding the transition.

Listen and Show Interest

As you engage in small talk, pay attention to your prospect's responses and show genuine interest in what they have to say. Nodding, smiling, and maintaining eye contact on a video call are nonverbal cues that indicate you're actively listening and engaged in the conversation.

I once was on a discovery call where I was the prospect. I tried to break the ice with a salesperson who was very stiff and didn't really want to engage. Every one of my attempts to break the ice fell flat. I was relatively young so I was kind, but I suddenly felt awkward and uncomfortable because it felt like the seller was not interested in pleasantries and just wanted to "get down to business." But just listening to the prospect and following their lead in conversation can help get the ball rolling.

Breaking the ice is all about establishing a connection and creating a comfortable environment for your discovery call. By being genuine, showing interest, and engaging in small talk, you'll set the stage for a more productive and pleasant conversation.

Remember that people are more likely to do business with those they like and trust, so building rapport from the start is key to a successful discovery call.

Setting the Agenda

Once you've passed the pleasantries in your discovery call, it's time to set the agenda. This isn't a formal agenda, but it helps give some structure to the call and lets you tell your prospect about your services without the awkwardness of a transition from discovery to presenting your offer.

When you don't set an agenda, it's easy for the call to get out of control and you find that you spend too much time in one place or run off tangent. This can result in a great conversation that leaves no time to present your offer.

In any sales interaction, you don't want to dominate the conversation; for the majority of the conversation, the prospect will be talking about their needs. Many sellers make the mistake of talking too much and missing the opportunity for the prospect to tell you how to sell to them.

An agenda for a call like this is quite simple. It can look like this:

Well, thanks for coming on the call with me—appreciate your time. So what I wanted to do is find out a bit more about you and your business, and then tell you a little about what we do and how we help our clients achieve X.

Does that work for you?

Timewise, are you okay till X?

Setting the agenda in an informal way demonstrates that you have respect for the prospects' time and that you are taking the conversation seriously without being too stiff and rigid. Likewise if you are giving clear intentions of how the conversation will go, you are also avoiding giving the prospect pitch shock when you present your offer to them. Your prospect is now expecting you to present your offer to them before the end of the call. The best part about sharing your intentions in this way is that it also removes the nervous energy from you thinking about pitching your offer because now your prospect is expecting it. You can drop the worries about how to talk about it or how to bring it up.

I always like to confirm the end time of the call, because if there is less time to do the call than I expect, I can still respect the hard deadline of the prospect. It also helps the prospect feel at ease because I am making clear that this will be done within the time agreed. A structure like this will help you and the prospect feel at ease and make your conversation flow more naturally.

Ultimately, the agenda is simply a tool to give structure to your call. If you adopt this into your sales calls, it will allow you to plan your calls better as you can prepare how you can present your offer.

Typically in a 30-minute discovery call, you devote around 15 minutes to the discovery and 10 minutes to presenting your offer and follow-up questions. I often find that a short discovery session will need a follow-up meeting. This leaves five minutes for breaking the ice and wrap-ups.

Having an agenda in this way will put you in control of the call's direction and help you follow a structure. Setting the agenda like this is especially important if you aren't a natural seller. Salespeople who live, eat, and sleep sales will do this instinctively, whereas if you are a reluctant seller, you will likely need to have a structure to keep you on track and avoid you going down rabbit holes that consume your time or distract the prospect from the value of your offer.

Discovery

You might be wondering why it's so essential to spend a significant portion of your discovery call asking questions. It's simple: the more you know about your prospect, the better positioned you are to offer a solution that truly resonates with their needs.

Sometimes, what a prospect believes they need isn't their most pressing problem. By asking probing questions, you're not just gathering data. You're encouraging introspection, prompting your prospect to think deeply about their current situation. This reflection often brings hidden challenges or desires to the forefront. And when you can address these underlying needs, your solution becomes even more compelling.

A generic sales pitch can feel impersonal and off the mark. But when you've gathered ample information about your prospect's specific situation, you can tailor your proposal to align perfectly with their requirements. This custom-tailored approach not only increases the chances of a successful conversion, but also makes your prospect feel heard and valued.

People love to talk about themselves, their businesses, and their challenges. By allowing your prospect to share their story and express their concerns, you're building a relationship. It's not just about understanding their needs; it's about establishing a connection, demonstrating empathy, and positioning yourself as someone genuinely interested in their success.

Every salesperson knows the challenge of objections. What if you could preemptively address them? By asking the right questions, you'll learn about any past solutions they've tried or any hesitations they might have. With this knowledge, you can proactively address these concerns when presenting your offer, eliminating potential roadblocks.

Your questions should also be a reflection of your industry knowledge. By posing insightful and thought-provoking questions, you're reinforcing the idea that you're not just a salesperson but an expert in your field. This expertise adds another layer of trust, ensuring your prospect feels confident in choosing your solution.

By diving deep into their needs and challenges, you can emphasize aspects of your solution that offer the most value to them. This not only showcases the benefits of your product or service, but also ensures your prospect understands precisely how they'll gain from partnering with you.

While you guide the conversation, it's the answers to your questions that dictate the direction. This subtle shift in dynamics makes the prospect feel empowered, like they're part of a collaborative process rather than just being sold to.

The questioning phase of a discovery call is more than just an information-gathering exercise. It's a strategy, an art of understanding, building trust, and subtly guiding your prospect toward realizing the value of your solution. It's about turning a conversation into a connection, and a lead into a loyal customer.

To excel in this phase, focus on active listening. It's not just about the questions you ask, but how you respond to the answers. Validate their concerns, offer insights where appropriate, and ensure that they feel heard.

Ultimately, a discovery call is a dance, a balance between guiding the conversation while allowing the prospect to lead. And it all starts with the right questions. The deeper you delve, the clearer the path becomes, paving the way for a successful partnership.

Questions for the Discovery Phase

During your discovery call you have limited time to get to the point. One of the big mistakes is to ask them to tell you about them and their company. If you ask this, it will likely end up in a 10-minute introduction, taking a big chunk of your time without really gaining you any discovery from the prospect.

So always start with "So what prompted you to book the call?" This helps me get to the point in an informal way and understand where they're coming from. This is always a good place to start. Once I've understood that, I can open up more questions and hey presto, we are into the discovery phase.

Here are some questions I use in my discovery calls:

- So, I've been doing a bit of research and understand you provide X, is that right?
- What prompted you to come on the call? What piqued your interest?
- Tell me a bit about where you are right now.
- What does success look like to you?

- What have you tried to reach your goal so far and how did it go?

- What do you think is holding you back from achieving [outcome]?

- If you could overcome the challenges and achieve [outcome], what would that do?

- How big a priority is that for you right now?

- Can you tell me more about your current situation/operation?

- What are the biggest challenges you are facing at the moment?

- How is this problem affecting your day-to-day operations?

- What would be the ideal outcome for you?

- How have you tried to address these issues so far?

- What is your main priority at this time?

- What are the consequences if these issues are not addressed?

- If you could wave a magic wand and have your ideal solution, what would it look like?

- What is the potential benefit if these issues are resolved?

- How soon would you like to start seeing improvements?

- What are the factors you consider when choosing a solution?

- Are there any specific features or services you are looking for in a solution?

- What kind of budget have you set aside for a solution like this?

- Who else on your team would be involved in the decision-making process?

- Can you walk me through your decision-making process?

- Are you considering other solutions or providers as well?

- How can we make our product/service a better fit for your needs?

- How do you feel our solution compares with other options you're considering?

- What obstacles, if any, do you foresee in implementing this solution?

- If we can meet your needs and work within your budget, are you prepared to move forward with this solution?

Mirroring Back

It's essential to realize that a great sales process isn't about manipulating a prospect, but about guiding them through a journey. Your job isn't just to sell, but to serve as a bridge between their needs and the solution you offer. To do this effectively, you need to resonate with what they've shared and present your solution in a manner that feels tailored and personal. Let's delve deeper into how you can achieve this.

The Art of Actively Mirroring Back

Imagine you're telling someone about a movie you watched. If they echo back a sentiment you shared, noting a specific scene you mentioned, you'd feel heard and understood, right? In sales, this technique is called "mirroring back." By reflecting a prospect's words, emotions, or concerns, you not only prove you were actively listening, but also create a connection.

When your prospect says, "We really need to improve sales this quarter," don't just note it down. Respond with, "I understand that boosting sales this quarter is a key priority for you. Let's explore how we can achieve that."

Every prospect has a unique history, having tried different solutions and faced varied challenges. When presenting your offer, home in on those specifics. If they mention having used a particular tool or service in the past without success, explain succinctly how your solution is distinct and addresses the gaps they experienced before.

For instance, if they say, "We tried digital advertising, but it didn't work for us," you could respond, "I understand your reservations given your past experience. Our approach to digital advertising is different because [specific unique selling proposition]."

Remember, every objection is an opportunity in disguise. If they're wary about a specific element, don't just gloss over it. Instead, address it directly or emphasize how your offer can be adapted to meet their unique preferences.

For example, if they mention not liking long-term contracts, you could either showcase a flexible plan or stress the benefits they'd derive from a long-term engagement with you.

A solution, no matter how great, loses its allure if it appears too complex. Assure your prospects by illustrating a straightforward onboarding or implementation process. Use phrases like, "It's just a three-step process," or "Our dedicated team will guide you through every phase, ensuring a smooth transition."

The outcome statement is the crux. It's the vision, the promised land. Always loop back to this. If you're selling a fitness program, for instance, and they want to lose weight, your outcome statement could be, "Imagine being 20 pounds lighter and feeling healthier than ever in just three months." Then, weave in your milestones and how your specific deliverables align to reach that outcome.

While it's crucial to highlight what they'll get (the deliverables), focus more on the transformative journey. The milestones are the stepping stones towards their ultimate goal. Paint a picture of how each milestone brings them closer to the desired outcome.

For instance, don't just say they'll get 12 coaching sessions (a deliverable). Express how by the fourth session, they'll develop healthier eating habits, and by the eighth, they'll be consistently hitting their weekly workout targets (milestones).

Once you've presented your offer, shift the spotlight back to them. Inviting questions isn't merely a formality; it's a sign you care about their thoughts and concerns. The more inquisitive they are, the deeper their interest. Remember, every question is an avenue to further tailor your solution to their needs.

Selling is an art, with the prospect at its center. By mirroring back, you establish rapport and trust. By presenting your offer in a prospect-centric way, you show them a vision of their future with your solution in it. Keep it simple, keep it focused, and always listen more than you speak. At the end of the day, your offer is not about what you're selling, but how it can transform your prospect's world.

Developing Your Mirroring Skills

Here are some key concepts and techniques that can help you when mirroring back:

- Before you can mirror, you need to truly listen. This means giving your undivided attention to your prospect, not formulating your next statement or pitch in your mind.

- If a prospect says, "We've had challenges with team collaboration," you might respond with, "I understand. So team collaboration has been a significant challenge?" This confirms understanding and often prompts the prospect to share more.

- Mirroring isn't just about words. If your prospect speaks slowly and deliberately, try to match that pace. If they're enthusiastic, mirror that energy. This creates a subtle synchronicity between you two.

- If a prospect uses specific terms or phrases, try to incorporate those terms into your responses. For instance, if they say they want a "user-friendly" solution, emphasize how your product is "extremely user-friendly."

- If you're unsure about something, mirror back with a request for more information. For instance, "You mentioned issues with your current software's efficiency. Can you expand on that?"

- If a prospect sounds frustrated or excited about something, acknowledge that emotion. "It sounds like that was a really frustrating experience for you."

- While mirroring often involves echoing exact words, you can occasionally paraphrase to ensure you've grasped the core idea. "So, if I understand correctly, you're looking for a solution that will not only be efficient but also scalable for your growing team?"

- Mirroring should feel natural, not forced. Don't try to mirror every statement or it might come off as inauthentic.

- After mirroring, validate their feelings or concerns. "I can see why that would be concerning for you."

- Like any skill, mirroring gets better with practice. Role-play with a colleague, simulate discovery calls, and get feedback.

- If you're on a video call, mirroring can extend to body language. If they lean forward when talking, you can do the same. If they use hand gestures frequently, you can occasionally incorporate similar gestures. It creates a subconscious feeling of similarity.

Remember, the aim isn't to parrot but to create a genuine connection. Always ensure your responses come from a place of genuine interest and understanding.

Presenting Your Offer

Choosing how to present your offer is a pivotal decision in the sales process. Let's explore the advantages and challenges of both the conversational and slide deck approaches, guiding you to discern which might be the best fit for your situation.

When you opt for a conversational delivery, you're tapping into the strength of personal connection. This method is rooted in building rapport with your prospect. There's an undeniable charm in the organic ebb and flow of a dialogue, fostering trust—critical in the decision-making process. Moreover, the dynamic nature of conversation grants you flexibility. You're in the driver's seat, adjusting your pitch in real time based on your prospect's reactions. If they express enthusiasm or raise concerns about a particular point, you can seamlessly tailor your message. The conversational style naturally invites participation and feedback, allowing the prospect to feel actively involved and valued. And there's an added bonus: amidst the routine of structured meetings, some prospects might find the informality of this approach refreshing.

However, the very freedom of conversation can sometimes be a double-edged sword. Without a framework, there's a possibility you might deviate from your central message, diluting the pitch's potency. There's also the inherent risk of missing out on emphasizing specific benefits or features of your offer. And while many appreciate a relaxed chat, some prospects might equate it with a lack of due preparation.

Contrastingly, using a slide deck offers a structured approach. With a slide deck, you're guaranteeing a clear and systematic delivery. Each slide serves as a beacon, guiding the discourse and ensuring all pivotal aspects of your offer are spotlighted. The visual nature of a slide deck can't be understated; humans are innately drawn to visuals. Thus, the imagery, graphs, and succinct bullet points can enhance clarity and appeal. Walking in with a polished slide deck also radiates professionalism—it speaks volumes about your preparation and commitment. And if you're pitching to various prospects, the reproducibility of a slide deck ensures uniformity across presentations.

But relying on a slide deck has its pitfalls. Overemphasis on slides can erect a virtual barrier between you and the prospect, making the interaction feel more like a monologue than a dialogue. And technology, for all its marvels, can occasionally betray us. A technical snag can interrupt the smooth flow of your pitch. The linear nature of slide decks can sometimes feel restrictive, especially if a prospect wishes to explore a point you planned for later in the sequence. Also, there lurks the temptation to overstuff slides with information, risking cognitive overload for the prospect.

To sum it up, both the conversational and slide deck methods have their distinct merits and challenges. Your choice should be a reflection of your offer's nature and the prospect's preferences. Consider the possibility of a hybrid approach, marrying the warmth of conversation with the clarity of a slide deck. Regardless of your chosen method, ensure you're attuned to your prospect's needs, making your offer resonate deeply with them.

Introducing Your Pricing

While both conversational and slide deck methods have their moments, when it comes to one of the most delicate aspects of the sales process—presenting your pricing—a slide deck can be an invaluable ally.

Discussing the financial aspect of your offer can be a touchy subject. You might find yourself grappling with a cocktail of emotions, from apprehension about the prospect's reaction to your own internal judgments about your offer's worth. This is especially true if you're not entirely comfortable with the price point, whether you feel it's too high or perhaps even too low.

Introducing pricing through a slide deck can help alleviate some of this discomfort. Here's why:

- **Structure and Context:** By the time you reach the pricing slide, you've already set the stage, emphasizing the value, benefits, and unique selling points of your offer. The price doesn't appear in isolation but in the context of the value it provides, making it easier to justify.

- **Visual Impact:** Sometimes, seeing numbers in a well-designed format, possibly alongside payment plans or bundled options, can make the price more digestible for both you and the prospect.

- **Creating a Buffer:** Directly stating the price can feel confrontational for some. Presenting it on a slide provides a brief moment of detachment, allowing the prospect to process the information before discussing it further.

- **Professionalism:** Much like other aspects of a slide deck, presenting pricing in this format can come across as professional and well thought out. It signals to the prospect that you've considered the pricing carefully and stand by its justification.

However, it's essential to ensure your slide isn't just about the price. It should effectively convey the value proposition. Remember, your prospect isn't just buying a product or service; they're investing in the outcomes and benefits it promises. Thus, when you present the price, it's not merely a number but the ticket to the transformation or solution you're offering.

Follow-Up Questions and Discussion

Once you have presented your offer, either formally or informally, you need to open up the discussion. This allows the prospect to ask questions and understand the offer in more detail. It's also where you can clarify their understanding and allay any concerns they might have. These questions, both from the prospect and from you, dive deeper into the heart of the matter, refining understanding and laying the groundwork for a successful collaboration.

After your pitch or presentation, it's imperative to open up for the prospect to ask questions. Just as the prospect may have questions about your offer, you should have questions for them. This two-way exchange ensures that both parties are on the same page and share mutual understanding.

When the prospect asks questions, it's a clear sign of engagement. They're trying to visualize the solution you're offering in their context. Responding promptly, confidently, and transparently to their queries will solidify their trust in you and your product.

Your queries should aim to clarify the prospect's position concerning your offer. It should help both of you understand if the solution is right for them. Here are some questions that can guide the conversation:

"Is this something that potentially could be a fit for you?"
This question gauges the prospect's initial reaction. It allows them to express any reservations or enthusiasm they might feel.
"How does that align with what you want to achieve?"
By asking this, you're urging the prospect to visualize the benefits of your offer in their context. It prompts them to think about the larger picture and how your solution fits into it.
"Do you have any thoughts on this?"
A more open-ended question, this offers the prospect a platform to voice opinions, concerns, or feedback, helping you better understand their mindset.

Scheduling Next Steps

The discovery call, an integral part of the sales process, is your golden ticket to dive deep into the needs, challenges, and aspirations of your prospects. But as with all good things, this call too must come to an end. Yet that conclusion should never be abrupt or leave matters hanging. Before you bid goodbye, ensuring clarity about the forthcoming steps is crucial. It keeps the momentum going, upholds professionalism, and positions you as a forward-thinking partner eager to drive results.

Never assume that a successful discovery call automatically translates into a secured deal. While you may have established a rapport and gained insights, the journey has only just begun. A follow-up meeting can serve as the perfect bridge between understanding their needs and presenting a tailored solution.

So, as you find the conversation winding down, channel your energy into shaping the road ahead. Here's how you can gracefully guide this transition:

- **Articulate Its Purpose:** Make sure your prospect knows the value of this subsequent interaction. For instance, you could say, "I'd love to have another chat after I've digested all the insights from our conversation today. This will allow me to present a solution that aligns perfectly with your needs."

- **Be Flexible with Timing:** Remember, your prospects are juggling multiple responsibilities. Offer a range of potential slots and ask about their preferred medium—whether that's a face-to-face meeting, a Zoom call, or a simple phone conversation. Every prospect is unique, and so is their timeline. Some may be in a hurry, seeking immediate solutions, while others could be in the initial stages of exploration, with months before any concrete decision. Your approach should respect and align with their timeline.

- **Craft with Care:** Sometimes, the next logical step is to draft a proposal detailing how you can address the issues or fulfill the desires highlighted during the discovery call. But sending a proposal and hoping they read it isn't enough. Your proposal should be a mirror, reflecting back what you've heard during the discovery call, tailored to demonstrate how you can address their specific pain points.

- **Preempt the Follow-Up:** When sending the proposal, don't leave its review to chance. Explicitly express your intention to discuss it, saying something like, "I'll send across a detailed proposal by Tuesday. How does Thursday afternoon sound for a quick call to walk you through it and address any questions?"

- **Ask Directly:** Simply inquire, "Could you share your expected timeline for making a decision?" or "What are your immediate priorities that we should keep in mind?" This not only showcases your respect for their pace but also helps you tailor your follow-up strategy.

- **Sync Your Solutions:** If a prospect is in urgent need, your proposal should reflect that urgency. Conversely, for those taking a more relaxed approach, offer value at regular intervals, ensuring you remain top-of-mind when they're ready to decide.

Here's one last point to ponder. While it's essential to guide the conversation towards actionable next steps, remember that a touch of authenticity goes a long way. Your prospects are more than just potential sales—they're individuals with aspirations, challenges, and stories. Your understanding and empathy towards their journey can be the differentiator not just in securing a deal but also in forging lasting relationships.

Fortune Is in the Follow-Up

We've all heard it said, "The fortune is in the follow-up," and this phrase carries more truth than most realize. No matter how positive a call feels, sealing a deal often requires more than one conversation.

Think of a successful call as planting a seed—it needs consistent care and attention before it can truly flourish.

Let's be clear: just because you had an enthusiastic chat doesn't mean your deal is in the bag. There's a vast chasm between interest and commitment. Many promising deals fade away, not due to a lack of interest, but simply because the seller didn't take the time to follow up. In the hustle and bustle of daily operations, it's easy for your proposal to get lost amid a sea of other pressing concerns in your prospect's world.

Remember, everyone's juggling numerous responsibilities and priorities. Sometimes, even if a prospect is keen on your proposal, it can slip their mind. They might set it aside with every intention to return, only to get swept up in another task. Your follow-up serves as a gentle reminder, a nudge, bringing your offer back into focus.

Moreover, in some scenarios, one follow-up might not cut it. Don't get disheartened. Multiple follow-ups might be the key to fortifying that bridge between interest and action. It's not always about the prospect being disinterested or deliberately avoiding; often, it's simply a matter of them being overwhelmed with other priorities.

So after that promising call, gear up for the next step. Consistent, tactful follow-up is where many sellers stumble, yet it's often where the real magic happens. Because, in sales as in life, persistence can make all the difference. Don't leave potential success on the table simply because you assumed a job was done; dive into the follow-up and discover the fortune that awaits.

Chapter 12

Mastering Your Mindset

For small business owners and solopreneurs, their business isn't just an enterprise; it's an extension of themselves. Every success feels personal, as does every setback. This deeply intertwined relationship between a business owner and their venture underscores the importance of mindset, especially when it comes to marketing and selling. But why is mindset such a linchpin?

The foundation of any successful marketing or sales endeavor is confidence. You're not merely peddling a product or a service; you're conveying value. You're presenting a solution, telling your potential customer that what you have can enrich their lives. However, confidence isn't something you can feign. If deep down you're unsure of your product's value, that hesitation will permeate your pitch, no matter how well crafted. A positive mindset instills a genuine belief in your offering, enabling you to communicate its worth passionately and convincingly.

But as any seasoned business person will attest, the journey is punctuated with challenges. Campaigns might not always hit their mark; pitches can be met with rejection. Here, mindset becomes the compass guiding your response. A resilient mindset reframes these setbacks as stepping stones, not stumbling blocks. It's the difference between being disheartened by a failed pitch and using it as a learning curve, adjusting your approach for the next time.

Establishing a Growth Mindset

At its core, a growth mindset is the belief that abilities and intelligence can be developed over time through dedication, hard work, and constructive feedback. It stands in contrast to a fixed mindset, which assumes that these traits are innate and immutable. Renowned psychologist Dr. Carol Dweck introduced the concept after decades of research on achievement and success. Her findings illuminated that the way we perceive our abilities profoundly affects our achievements.

Individuals with a growth mindset tend to embrace challenges, persevere through obstacles, and see effort as a natural part of the learning journey. They're more likely to learn from criticism and be inspired by the success of others. When faced with failure, instead of resigning to the belief that "I'm just not good at this," they more often think, "I need a different approach, or I need to put in more effort."

In comparison, those with a fixed mindset may avoid challenges for fear of failure, give up quickly when faced with obstacles, and may feel threatened by others' successes. They often believe that if they're truly talented or intelligent, things should come easily to them, and if they don't, it's a reflection of their inherent incapabilities.

A growth mindset cultivates a love for learning. Individuals become more resilient in the face of setbacks, viewing them not as insurmountable failures but as opportunities to learn and adapt. This resilience enables them to overcome challenges that may deter others.

By believing that effort plays a significant role in success, people with a growth mindset are more likely to put in the necessary work, pushing themselves harder and further. Constructive criticism becomes a tool for growth rather than a source of discouragement. This openness to feedback can significantly accelerate personal and professional development.

Recognizing that everyone is on a journey of growth and that abilities aren't fixed can foster better interpersonal relationships. There's less competition and more collaboration, because individuals are less threatened by others' successes and more inspired by them. While a fixed mindset might bring success in the short term, especially if one relies heavily on existing talents, a growth mindset is more conducive to long-term success. It allows individuals to adapt, evolve, and navigate the challenges that inevitably arise.

The implications of having a growth mindset extend beyond personal achievements. It's transformative in education, professional settings, and personal relationships. Teachers and parents who understand the growth mindset can cultivate environments where children aren't limited by perceived innate abilities but are encouraged to explore, make mistakes, and learn.

Practical Tips for Building Your Mindset

There are a number of ways you can develop and strengthen your mindset:

- **Embrace Challenges:** Instead of avoiding challenges, view them as opportunities to learn and grow. Remember, every obstacle you overcome adds to your experience and resilience.

- **Celebrate Small Wins:** It's important to recognize and celebrate small achievements. These moments can be foundational in building confidence and reinforcing a growth mindset.

- **Learn from Failures:** Instead of ruminating on setbacks, analyze them. What went wrong? How can you approach it differently next time? By learning from your mistakes, you turn them into stepping stones for future success.

- **Stay Curious:** Foster a natural curiosity. Ask questions, seek out new experiences, and embrace lifelong learning. This helps keep your mind open and adaptable.

- **Avoid Comparing Yourself to Others:** Everyone's on their own unique journey. Comparing yourself to others can create unnecessary stress and can skew your perception. Focus on your own growth and progress.

- **Value Effort over Talent:** Recognize that consistent effort often trumps raw talent. It's not just about innate abilities but about dedication, persistence, and hard work.

- **Seek Constructive Feedback:** Don't shy away from feedback. Constructive criticism can provide invaluable insights and perspectives that foster growth. Be open and receptive, even if it's tough to hear.

- **Replace Negative Thoughts:** When you catch yourself thinking "I can't do this," try adding "yet" to the end. This simple addition can shift your perspective from a fixed mindset to a growth mindset.

- **Surround Yourself with Growth-Minded Individuals:** Being around people who encourage and challenge you can significantly influence your mindset. Their attitudes and outlooks can be contagious and supportive.

- **Set Clear Goals:** Break down large goals into smaller, actionable steps. This makes them more manageable and provides a clear path for growth and progress.

- **Practice Self-Compassion:** Understand that it's okay to have setbacks. Be kind to yourself and recognize that every individual, no matter how successful, faces challenges. What matters is how you respond and bounce back.

Adaptability is gold. Strategies that were once the gold standard can quickly become passé. Enter the growth mindset: an outlook that not only adapts to change but embraces it. With this mindset, you're not playing catchup; you're at the forefront, leveraging new avenues and opportunities as they emerge.

Beyond strategies and campaigns, sales are built on relationships, especially for smaller businesses. Trust is the currency. When you approach your prospects with a genuine mindset, focused not just on sales but on understanding and delivering value, you lay the foundation for lasting business relationships. This isn't about one-off transactions; it's about cultivating trust, which translates into loyalty, repeat business, and referrals.

However, it's also crucial to touch upon the pitfalls of a negative mindset. Such a mindset can magnify every rejection, making it feel deeply personal. It can lead to undervaluing your services, stemming from a misplaced belief that lowering prices is the only way to clinch a sale. It breeds excessive caution, which might mean missed opportunities. And perhaps most damagingly, it can result in sporadic, inconsistent efforts, which can hamper brand growth.

For small business owners and solopreneurs, it's the sail that steers the ship. It shapes actions, determines responses, and influences outcomes. In the realm of marketing and sales, where every pitch and campaign counts, having the right mindset isn't just beneficial; it's pivotal. Remember, when the mind is geared towards positivity, potential, and growth, the path to success becomes not just clearer but also more attainable.

Self-Doubt Is Normal

Amid the myriad challenges that come with being a small business owner or solopreneur, one of the most profound yet least discussed is the internal battle: confronting and conquering your own self-doubt.

It's an experience that's as universal as it is personal. Every entrepreneur, no matter how seasoned, grapples with moments of uncertainty and hesitation. These feelings are not just common; they're a natural part of the entrepreneurial journey. However, recognizing their existence is the first step towards mastering them.

Self-doubt often stems from our innate desire for validation and fear of failure. When you're at the helm of your business, the stakes are higher. Every decision, every move is a reflection of you. This pressure can amplify feelings of uncertainty. Questions like "Am I good enough?" "Is my product or service truly valuable?" or "What if I fail?" can become constant companions.

However, there's a silver lining to these feelings of doubt. They're a testament to your investment in your business, both emotionally and practically. They signify that you care deeply about the outcome. Yet while these feelings are natural, they needn't be debilitating.

Conquering Self-Doubt

To conquer self-doubt, start by acknowledging it. Understand that every entrepreneur, from the one starting a local cafe to the one launching a tech startup, has moments of hesitation. These feelings aren't indicative of your capability or worth; they're simply part of the human experience.

Next, consider maintaining a record of your achievements. It might sound simple, but having a tangible list of milestones, big or small, can be a powerful antidote to moments of uncertainty. Whenever doubt creeps in, revisit this list. It serves as a reminder of your journey, your growth, and your capabilities.

Engaging with a supportive community can also be invaluable. This could be fellow entrepreneurs, business mentors, or even supportive friends and family. Sharing your feelings and hearing others' experiences can provide perspective. You'll often find that your fears and doubts are echoed by many, and there's solace in knowing you're not alone.

Lastly, consider reframing your mindset. Instead of viewing challenges or setbacks as affirmations of your doubts, view them as growth opportunities. Every hiccup is a chance to learn, adapt, and evolve. When you start viewing challenges through this lens, they become less intimidating. Instead of being roadblocks, they transform into stepping stones.

Feelings of self-doubt and uncertainty are par for the course in the entrepreneurial journey. They're as much a part of the process as the highs of success. However, with the right mindset, tools, and support, these feelings can be navigated and even harnessed for personal and professional growth. Remember, in the vast tapestry of your business journey, moments of doubt are mere threads, not defining patterns.

Replacing Inaction with Action

As a small business owner or solopreneur, you've probably consumed countless books, webinars, and seminars, absorbing a trove of knowledge. But no matter how extensive, knowledge remains abstract until it's given life through action. The genuine essence of learning—the kind that brings about transformative growth—isn't in the acquisition of information but in its application.

Imagine a musician who understands every nuance of music theory but never touches an instrument, or a chef who knows the intricacies of culinary arts on paper but never steps into the kitchen. Without implementation, their knowledge remains dormant, never truly coming to life. The same holds true for business. Your ideas, strategies, and plans only become tangible and real when you act upon them. It's in the trenches of the real world, amid successes and setbacks, that true learning happens.

Yet for many, taking that step into the realm of action is daunting. The quest for perfection often becomes a significant roadblock. While striving for excellence is commendable, pursuing absolute perfection is not only unrealistic but can be paralyzing. Perfectionism, at its core, is rooted in fear—the fear of making mistakes, the fear of judgment, or even the fear of success. However, chasing this elusive ideal can stall progress. In waiting for that "perfect" moment or that "flawless" plan, you might miss out on invaluable opportunities to learn, adapt, and grow.

Taking action, even if imperfectly, propels you forward. Each step, whether it leads to success or presents a challenge, becomes a lesson. These real-world experiences provide insights no textbook or seminar can offer. They refine your strategies, hone your skills, and mold you into a more resilient entrepreneur.

The fear of failure is a sentiment every business owner grapples with. It's a natural human instinct to avoid situations where failure is a possibility. However, it's essential to reframe our understanding of failure. Instead of viewing it as a definitive end, see it as a pit stop on your journey—a place where you reassess, learn, and pivot. Every renowned entrepreneur or business magnate has tales of failures, but what sets them apart is their perspective. They viewed these setbacks not as roadblocks but as stepping stones.

The irony is that the most significant failure of all is inaction. When you don't act due to fear, you've already let failure win. It's a passive acceptance of defeat without even stepping onto the battlefield. Conversely, taking action, even with the risk of failure, keeps the doors to possibilities open.

I've had plans and ideas sitting in a notepad for years, some of them I started with enthusiasm and then talked myself out of them with negative self-talk. I've also fallen victim to the "I'll just learn this," which becomes an excuse for not being emotionally and mentally invested in an idea or project. We don't want to fail, and sometimes (especially for me) learning more stuff becomes an excuse for avoiding the risk of failing. Everything fails, if we don't make a decision to make it work. When I launched my educational events, the first event I had was a big room and a handful of people. It was embarrassing. The second time around, I worked that bit harder and got a bigger crowd. Three months later, I was packing the rooms. We don't get success without risk, effort, and commitment to an outcome. As we go we'll hit roadblocks, make mistakes, and learn things, but we keep making progress.

In my live training events, I share a lot of practical strategies, but the number one thing people struggle with is their mindset—their thinking gets in the way of the result. My motto is "Nothing works out of the box." That means you need to commit to a journey to building a plan and making it work. Adjust the sails, but not the destination.

Inaction is often a silent killer of dreams. It allows doubt, procrastination, and fear to fester, undermining your confidence and resolve. On the other hand, taking action, even in small, incremental steps, builds momentum. With each step, you gain more clarity, confidence, and conviction. You learn, you adapt, and most importantly, you grow.

Knowledge is your compass, but action is your vehicle. Without the latter, the former remains static, never truly realizing its potential. Embrace the journey with all its uncertainties. Let go of the shackles of perfectionism and lean into the lessons that come with every step. Celebrate your successes, learn from your setbacks, but most importantly, keep moving forward. In the dynamic dance of entrepreneurship, it's momentum, fueled by consistent action, that leads to lasting success.

Chapter 13

Tactics and Resources to Take Your Business to the Next Level

In this chapter, we'll explore different approaches and resources you can use to really expand on everything you've learned.

How to Write Content for Any Social Media Platform

Social media content follows a similar pattern across all the different channels. This works across any social media channel and any format. It breaks down into these sections:

- **The Hook:** In order to stop people from scrolling, you need to say, show, or do something that gives them a compelling reason to give you the 10 seconds.

- **The Teaser:** Within the next 10 seconds, you should be giving the viewer a compelling reason to read or watch to the end by means of some promise of reward for the time invested.

- **Substance:** For the remainder of the video, you should be working with the objective of delivering on the promise of value and giving the viewer an emotional reaction from the content. This is an emotional reaction that has made it worth their time to watch or read what you had to offer. These emotional reactions can involve, among other things, anger, sadness, laughter, fascination, inspiration, and realization.

- **Wrap Up:** Before you finish the post, remind the viewer how this can make a difference to them.

- **Call to Action:** At the end of all this, you should leave with a call to action. Tell them clearly what you want them to do next.

90 Days of Social Media Content

In today's digital age, social media has become an essential tool for businesses to connect with their audience and build their brand presence. However, consistently coming up with fresh and engaging content can be a challenge. That's why I've compiled a list of 90 social media content ideas that can work for any business, regardless of industry or niche.

With these content ideas, you'll have a wealth of inspiration to keep your social media channels active and captivating. From sharing behind-the-scenes glimpses of your business to providing valuable tips and insights, this diverse range of content will help you connect with your audience, drive engagement, and ultimately grow your online presence.

Feel free to mix and match, experiment with different formats, and put your own spin on these ideas to create content that resonates with your target audience. Remember, social media is an opportunity to showcase your expertise, build trust with your audience, and foster meaningful connections. It's not just about promoting your products or services, but also providing value and engaging with your community. By leveraging these content ideas, you'll be able to create a dynamic and compelling social media presence that keeps your audience coming back for more.

So, whether you're looking for inspiration for your next Instagram post, LinkedIn poll, Facebook update, or X thread, this list of 90 content ideas will serve as a valuable resource to fuel your creativity and help you craft engaging and impactful social media content:

1. Introduce your team members and share fun facts about them.
2. Share a customer success story or testimonial.
3. Post a behind-the-scenes photo or video of your workspace.
4. Share a motivational quote related to your industry.
5. Conduct a poll or survey to gather insights from your audience.
6. Share a quick tip or hack related to your product or service.
7. Highlight a feature or benefit of your product/service.
8. Share an interesting statistic or industry fact.
9. Post a throwback photo or memory related to your business.
10. Recommend a book or resource that your audience might find valuable.
11. Share a fun fact about your industry or niche.
12. Run a contest or giveaway on your social media channels.
13. Post a before-and-after photo or transformation related to your business.
14. Share a testimonial or review from a satisfied customer.
15. Ask your audience to share their favorite product or service from your business.
16. Post a funny or relatable meme related to your industry.
17. Share a tutorial or step-by-step guide on how to use your product.
18. Celebrate a milestone or anniversary for your business.
19. Post a photo or video showcasing your product in action.
20. Share a success tip or productivity hack for your audience.

Tactics and Resources to Take Your Business to the Next Level

21. Highlight a charitable cause or community initiative your business supports.

22. Post a trivia question related to your industry and offer a prize for the correct answer.

23. Share a customer spotlight and highlight their achievements.

24. Post a behind-the-scenes photo or video of a recent project or event.

25. Share a fun fact or interesting piece of history about your business.

26. Invite your audience to ask questions and host a live Q&A session.

27. Share a testimonial or review from a happy client.

28. Post a motivational or inspiring video related to your industry.

29. Feature a partner or collaborator and showcase their work.

30. Share a quick tip for improving a specific aspect of your audience's life or work.

31. Post a quote from a thought leader in your industry.

32. Share a customer testimonial in the form of a video or audio clip.

33. Highlight a lesser-known feature or benefit of your product/service.

34. Post a "Did You Know?" fact related to your industry or niche.

35. Share a behind-the-scenes photo or video of your product being made.

36. Recommend a podcast or YouTube channel your audience might enjoy.

37. Post a photo or video of your team participating in a team-building activity.

38. Share a case study showcasing the results and impact of your product/service.

39. Ask your audience for feedback or suggestions on how to improve your offering.

40. Share a success story or achievement of your business.

41. Post a fun and engaging quiz related to your industry or niche.

42. Share a customer review or testimonial in the form of a visual quote.

43. Highlight a feature or benefit of your product/service through a short video.

44. Post a photo or video showcasing your product/service in a creative setting.

45. Share a productivity tip or time-saving hack for your audience.

46. Recommend a relevant app or tool that can benefit your audience.

47. Post a before-and-after transformation related to your product or service.

48. Share a behind-the-scenes look at your creative process or design inspiration.

49. Ask your audience to share their favorite ways to use your product/service.

50. Highlight a team member's expertise or area of specialization.

51. Post a quick and easy recipe or DIY project related to your industry.

52. Share a success story or milestone achieved by one of your customers.

53. Feature a customer or client and share their experience with your business.

Tactics and Resources to Take Your Business to the Next Level

54. Post a fun and interactive quiz or puzzle for your audience to solve.

55. Share a customer review or testimonial in the form of a written story.

56. Highlight a unique feature or aspect of your product/service through visuals.

57. Post a behind-the-scenes photo or video of a recent event or trade show.

58. Share a personal story or anecdote related to your business journey.

59. Recommend a relevant blog or article that your audience might find informative.

60. Post a photo or video showcasing the craftsmanship or attention to detail in your product.

61. Share a tip for overcoming a common challenge in your industry.

62. Host a live tutorial or demonstration of your product/service.

63. Highlight a customer or client's success and the role your product/service played.

64. Post a funny or relatable comic strip related to your industry.

65. Share a quick and easy DIY project using your product/service.

66. Feature a team member and share their favorite industry-related book or resource.

67. Post a photo or video of your product/service being used in a unique or unexpected way.

68. Share a customer review or testimonial in the form of a video interview.

69. Highlight a key industry trend or development and provide your insights.

70. Post a behind-the-scenes photo or video of your product/service being tested or quality checked.

71. Recommend a relevant documentary or film that your audience might find interesting.

72. Share a success tip or advice for entrepreneurs or professionals in your industry.

73. Host a live webinar or workshop on a topic of interest to your audience.

74. Highlight a customer or client and share their journey and progress with your business.

75. Post a funny or entertaining video related to your industry.

76. Share a quick and easy self-care or wellness tip for your audience.

77. Feature a partner or collaborator and showcase a joint project or initiative.

78. Post a photo or video of your team participating in a volunteer or community service activity.

79. Share a customer review or testimonial in the form of an infographic or visual presentation.

80. Highlight a customer or client's transformation and the impact your product/service had on their life.

81. Post a motivational quote or message related to personal or professional growth.

82. Recommend a relevant TED Talk or conference talk that your audience might find inspiring.

83. Share a behind-the-scenes photo or video of your product being packaged or shipped.

Tactics and Resources to Take Your Business to the Next Level

84. Ask your audience to share their favorite tips or advice related to your industry.

85. Highlight a team member's favorite industry-related podcast or YouTube channel.

86. Post a photo or video showcasing your product/service being used in a unique location or setting.

87. Share a customer review or testimonial in the form of a visual collage.

88. Host a live panel discussion with industry experts or thought leaders.

89. Share a quick and easy DIY maintenance or troubleshooting tip for your product/service.

90. Feature a customer or client and share their journey from start to success with your business.

Feel free to adapt and modify these ideas to fit your business and audience. The key is to provide valuable, engaging, and relevant content that resonates with your target audience and encourages interaction and conversation.

20 Marketing Ideas to Grow Your Business

It can be a challenge to come up with ideas from scratch, especially when it's your own business. At many times in my career I've had a "why didn't I think of that moment." Sometimes you just need a starting idea that you can tweak and make your own.

For any idea, you'll need to have a plan, take action, and improve as you go. I've put together 20 ideas anyone can start right now. You don't need to do them all; pick a couple and get really good at them.

Remember, good things come to those who are consistent.

1. **Start a Podcast:** Create your own podcast where you can share valuable industry insights, expertise, and engaging conversations with your target audience. Podcasts allow you to establish thought leadership, reach a wider audience, and build a loyal community of listeners. Research podcasting equipment, recording and editing techniques, and topics that resonate with your target market.

2. **Podcast Guest:** Leverage the popularity of podcasts by being a guest on other shows within your industry. This allows you to tap into existing audiences and showcase your expertise to a new set of listeners. Research relevant podcasts, reach out to hosts, and propose topics that align with their audience and your expertise.

3. **X:** Engage with your audience through short, timely messages on X. Share industry news, insights, and updates about your business. Use relevant hashtags, participate in conversations, and follow industry leaders and influencers to expand your network and increase your visibility.

4. **Facebook:** Connect with your community through posts and updates on your business's Facebook page. Share informative content, behind-the-scenes glimpses, and engage in conversations with your followers. Utilize Facebook groups and ads to reach a wider audience and promote your products or services.

5. **LinkedIn:** Build professional relationships and establish yourself as an industry expert on LinkedIn. Share industry news, thought-provoking articles, and professional insights. Connect with colleagues, join relevant groups, and engage with others' content to expand your network and create valuable connections.

6. **YouTube:** Create and share videos on YouTube to showcase your expertise and provide valuable content to your audience. Create tutorials, product demonstrations, or educational videos related to your industry. Optimize your videos with keywords and engaging thumbnails to increase visibility and reach.

7. **YouTube Shorts:** Tap into the popularity of short-form video content with YouTube Shorts. Create vertical videos under 60 seconds that are entertaining, informative, or visually engaging. Use trending hashtags and participate in challenges to increase your visibility and attract a wider audience.

8. **TikTok:** Utilize the viral nature of short-form video content on TikTok to showcase your brand, products, or services. Create engaging, creative, and entertaining videos that resonate with your target audience. Use popular sounds, trends, and hashtags to increase the chances of your content going viral.

9. **Lead Magnets:** Offer valuable resources such as e-books, guides, templates, or checklists in exchange for your audience's contact details. These lead magnets help you build an email list and establish trust with potential customers. Create high-quality, informative resources that address specific pain points or challenges your audience may have.

10. **Webinars:** Host online presentations or workshops on topics relevant to your audience. Webinars allow you to showcase your expertise, engage with participants, and generate leads. Choose engaging presentation formats, use interactive tools, and provide actionable takeaways to keep participants interested and provide value.

11. **In-Person Events:** Organize your own in-person events such as workshops, seminars, or networking sessions. These events provide an opportunity to connect directly with potential customers, showcase your products or services, and establish personal relationships. Consider the logistics, venue, and promotion to create a memorable and valuable experience for attendees.

12. **Trade Shows:** Exhibit at industry trade shows to reach a wider market and connect with potential customers. Trade shows allow you to showcase your products or services, network with industry professionals, and generate leads. Research relevant trade shows, plan your booth design, and prepare engaging promotional materials to increase your impact.

13. **Networking:** Attend industry events, conferences, or join professional groups to network with peers, industry experts, and potential customers. Build relationships, exchange ideas, and explore collaboration opportunities. Be prepared with your elevator pitch and genuine interest in learning from others.

14. **Direct Mail:** Send targeted promotional materials via traditional mail to reach your audience in a more tangible way. Direct mail can include post cards, brochures, or catalogues. Develop a compelling design and messaging, ensure accurate targeting, and track the effectiveness of your direct mail campaigns.

15. **Competitions:** Run contests or giveaways to generate excitement and engage with your audience. Competitions can include social media challenges, photo contests, or random draws. Set clear rules, establish attractive prizes, and promote the competition through various channels to increase participation.

16. **Blogging:** Create informative and engaging blog posts on topics relevant to your industry or target audience. Share your expertise, provide valuable insights, and address common pain points. Optimize your blog posts for search engines, share them on social media, and encourage discussions in the comments section.

17. **Press Release and Local News:** Issue press releases to local media outlets and share newsworthy updates about your business. This helps you gain media coverage, reach a broader audience, and enhance your brand visibility. Research local media contacts, craft attention-grabbing press releases, and follow up with journalists for potential coverage.

18. **Speaking at Events:** Present at conferences, industry events, or local gatherings to showcase your expertise and establish yourself as a thought leader. Speaking engagements provide opportunities to connect with a captive audience, share valuable insights, and build credibility. Research relevant events, propose engaging topics, and prepare impactful presentations.

19. **Email Marketing:** Build relationships and promote your business through targeted email marketing campaigns. Develop a well-segmented email list, craft personalized and engaging emails, and provide valuable content to your subscribers. Use email automation tools to streamline your campaigns and track their effectiveness.

20. **Referral Programs:** Encourage your existing customers to refer others to your business through referral programs. Offer incentives, discounts, or rewards for successful referrals. Develop a clear referral process, communicate the benefits to customers, and track referrals to reward loyal customers who bring in new business.

21 Sites and Tools You Should Check Out

As we embark on the journey through the digital landscape of today's entrepreneurial ecosystem, we are met with an array of tools and platforms designed to streamline our processes, amplify our presence, and fuel our growth. Whether it's enhancing the visibility of our brand, communicating with customers, managing our projects, or processing payments, the right tools are crucial for efficiency and success. This section of the book is dedicated to arming you with a curated list of valuable websites and tools that can significantly propel your business forward.

Navigating the digital sphere can be overwhelming, especially for small business owners juggling numerous tasks simultaneously. The internet is awash with a plethora of tools, each promising to be the magic wand that will transform your business overnight. However, not all tools are created equal, and discerning the right ones for your specific needs is crucial. This section will not only provide you with a compilation of tried-and-tested tools but also offer insights into their applications and optimal usage, so you can make informed decisions based on your business's unique requirements.

The digital resources featured in this section have been carefully selected for their proven track records and reliable performance. From user-friendly website builders to intuitive email marketing platforms, comprehensive analytics tools, and secure payment gateways, you'll find an array of options tailored to your specific needs. Whether you're just getting started or looking to scale your operations, these tools will provide the support and automation you need to achieve your goals.

Each tool is accompanied by a brief description and a link to its website, making it easy for you to explore further and get started. Moreover, we'll delve into practical use cases, real-world applications,

Tactics and Resources to Take Your Business to the Next Level

and helpful tips to get the full benefit of these tools, ensuring you can make the most of your digital investments:

1. **Google Analytics:** Web analytics service that tracks and reports website traffic, helping businesses understand their audience: https://analytics.google.com/

2. **Mailchimp:** Marketing automation platform and email marketing service to create, send, and analyze email campaigns: https://mailchimp.com/

3. **Hootsuite:** Social media management platform to schedule, publish, and analyze social media content across multiple networks: https://hootsuite.com/

4. **HubSpot:** Inbound marketing, sales, and customer service platform with tools for content management, CRM, and analytics: https://www.hubspot.com/

5. **Canva:** Graphic design tool to create a variety of content, including social media graphics, presentations, and flyers: https://www.canva.com/

6. **Yoast SEO:** WordPress plugin that provides search engine optimization (SEO) tools to improve website visibility in search engines: https://yoast.com/

7. **SEMrush:** Online visibility and marketing analytics platform with tools for SEO, PPC, content, social media, and competitive research: https://www.semrush.com/

8. **Buffer:** Social media management platform for scheduling and publishing posts, tracking performance, and engaging with the audience: https://buffer.com/

9. **Ahrefs:** SEO toolset to review website performance, track keywords, perform competitive analysis, and more: https://ahrefs.com/

10. **Trello:** Collaboration tool that organizes projects into boards, lists, and cards, helping teams stay organized and on track: https://trello.com/

11. **Constant Contact:** Email marketing automation platform with customizable templates, contact management, and reporting tools: https://www.constantcontact.com/

12. **Zapier:** Automation tool that connects and automates tasks between different apps, streamlining workflows and saving time: https://zapier.com/

13. **SurveyMonkey:** Online survey development platform that helps businesses gather feedback and insights from their audience: https://www.surveymonkey.com/

14. **Moz:** SEO software and data to help businesses optimize their websites, track rankings, and improve organic traffic: https://moz.com/

15. **Sprout Social:** Social media management platform for scheduling, publishing, and analyzing content, and engaging with the audience: https://sproutsocial.com/

16. **Stripe:** Online payment processing for internet businesses, allowing businesses to accept payments, manage subscriptions, and handle other financial transactions: https://stripe.com/

17. **Wix:** Website builder that allows users to create responsive websites using drag-and-drop functionality, templates, and customization features: https://www.wix.com/

18. **Gumroad:** Online platform that enables creators to sell products directly to consumers, including digital products, subscriptions, and physical goods: https://gumroad.com/

Tactics and Resources to Take Your Business to the Next Level

19. **Leadpages:** Online tool that provides templates and features for creating high-converting landing pages, pop-ups, and alert bars to capture leads: https://www.leadpages.net/

20. **Kajabi:** All-in-one platform for creating, marketing, and selling online courses and membership sites: https://kajabi.com/

21. **CapCut:** A free all-in-one video editing app that offers a variety of editing tools, effects, and filters for creating professional-quality videos. It's popular among social media creators and influencers: https://www.capcut.net/

Chapter 14

It's Time for Action

We've reached the final chapter. Now it's time to take action.

There will always be a reason not to market. There will always be a reason something needs more work. But you only grow when you take steps.

Your actions will determine your future.

I once consulted with a small video firm in Bristol, England, that was struggling to get new clients onboard. They'd launched numerous marketing campaigns and had lots of conversations but they weren't translating to growth and winning clients.

I spent two days reviewing their business and asking questions. As I studied their business, I spotted that all the components of success were in place, but they were not joining them up. Everything was there, but not in a systemized way. Marketing was erratic and the process of closing a client through a discovery call wasn't aligned.

Over the course of a few months, I guided them through the concepts and principles I've shared in this book. The success wasn't overnight, but as they implemented the changes step by step, they saw marginal improvements.

Over six months, those marginal improvements saw their close rate on new business go from 2 in 10 to 6 in 10. These little improvements and consistent approach brought them more inquiries and helped them win more of them.

That's the power contained in this book when it's implemented. To your success!

Acknowledgments

Whoa, I did this, I'm sitting writing the acknowledgments for my first book. If you'd have asked 17-year-old Dean if he'd write a book, he'd 110% tell you it would never happen for this college dropout with working-class roots.

It shows how much you can grow and achieve if you work at it, despite all the problems, fears, and lack of resources. But the book is not just a journey for you; it's the lessons I've learned along the way. They're my lessons.

I could write a long list of people I need to thank, but I'm sure I'd leave someone out. There are many people who've been there for me and helped along my journey—the journey that is now documented in the lessons of this book.

So I want to thank everyone, but there is one person I want to thank ahead of them all: my dad.

He worked flat out to provide for me and give me the best chance in life. He was always working away in the background to look after us. He backed me to the hilt starting my business too and supported me when I had my tail between my legs.

He is part of the generation that doesn't make a fuss and gets on with things, so this is my way of putting on record that he is the best dad anyone could have.

He is the hero of our family.

Dad, I know we don't do soppy emotions, but thank you.

About the Author

Dean Seddon (https://maverrik.io/, https://www.deanseddon.io/; Plymouth, UK) is the founder of Maverrik, the UK's fastest-growing business growth consultancy. Having delivered growth in several small and large businesses, he embarked on building an organization that would help businesses cut through the fog and grow people, sales, and profits. Dean is a practical, hands-on business speaker and trainer. Supported by the Maverrik team, Dean speaks at over 100 events per year, consults with large and small businesses across the world, and is passionate about getting results for people.

Index

231

241

Index